T. S. Eliot was born in St. Louis in 1888, and educated at Harvard, the Sorbonne, and at Merton College, Oxford. Although his first poems were published as early as 1909, it was not until the appearance of PRUFROCK AND OTHER OBSERVATIONS in 1917 that his verse began to receive general recognition. Harvard, Princeton, and Yale are among the many universities which have conferred honorary degrees upon him, and in 1948 he received the Nobel Prize, as well as one of the British Empire's highest awards, the Order of Merit.

T. S. ELIOT

Essays on Elizabethan Drama

A HARVEST BOOK
Harcourt, Brace & World, Inc.
New York

IN MEMORIAM
DONALD BRACE

Preface

When it was suggested that I should make, for inclusion in the Harvest series, a selection of essays from the selection of my essays published under the title of *Selected Essays,* my first thought was to reprint a small selection published many years ago in England, called *Elizabethan Essays.* With this aim in view, it seemed prudent to reread these essays, at most of which I had not looked, I suspect, since I read the proof for that book. The result was somewhat surprising.

Two of the essays were concerned with Shakespeare: *Shakespeare and the Stoicism of Seneca* and *Hamlet and His Problems.* A third was entitled *Four Elizabethan Dramatists* with the somewhat pretentious subtitle "Preface to an Unwritten Book." All three of these essays on re-examination embarrassed me by their callowness, and by a facility of unqualified assertion which verges, here and there, on impudence. The *Hamlet,* of course, had been kept afloat all these years by the success of the phrase "objective correlative"—a phrase which, I am now told, is not even my own but was first used by Washington

Alston. These three essays were the first to be reread; and when I had read them I turned with trepidation to reread my essays on Shakespeare's contemporaries. I was astonished to find that these essays struck me as very good indeed.

What is the reason for my forming such different judgments on different essays? I believe that the explanation is at least partly to be found in the fact that Shakespeare is so much greater than any of his contemporaries. About Marlowe, or Ford, or even Ben Jonson, it is possible for a young man (and I was a very young man, or an immature youngish man, when I wrote these essays) to have something to say with which he will still find himself in agreement thirty years or more later. It may even be that a youthful sensibility is the most desirable qualification for writing about these minor poets and dramatists. Mature wisdom, and much experience of men and books, is perhaps unnecessary for the appreciation of their work. But, for the understanding of Shakespeare, a lifetime is not too long; and of Shakespeare, the development of one's opinions may be the measure of one's development in wisdom.

However this may be, I have rejected these three essays in compiling this book. Instead, I have included *Seneca in Elizabethan Translation,* which seems to me to deserve its place as the first "essay in Elizabethan drama." Like the other essays, it contains some good quotations. And that perhaps is another reason why it is easier to write about minor Elizabethan and Jacobean drama than about Shakespeare: an essay can be worth reading for the quotations alone. Quotations from Shakespeare are too well known; it is not enough to quote well; the critic must have something worth saying about his quotations from Shakespeare.

I call the attention of students of Elizabethan drama to the fact that the date of each essay is given in the Table of Contents. This is a practice I like to observe in printing any collection of essays; but it is peculiarly important where the critical judgments may depend on the conclusions of current scholarship. It may well be that later scholarly research has disproved assumptions which I then accepted. On the other hand, if in discussing any dramatist I have ignored any work of scholarship with which I should have been acquainted when I wrote about him, I shall expect my criticism to be marked down accordingly.

On the whole, I think that these essays do provide a helpful introduction to the study of the poetic drama of the age of Elizabeth I and James I, and to the very interesting differentia of temperament and technique between the dramatists. There are two conspicuous omissions. I do not so much regret the absence of an essay on the work of John Webster: a great deal has been written on this subject, two of his plays are very well known and are from time to time performed, and I have alluded constantly to Webster in discussing other dramatists. But I very much regret the fact that I did not, during that period of my life at which these essays were written, have occasion to write about the work of that very great poet and dramatist, George Chapman. It is too late now: to attempt to repair such a gap, after many years' neglect, would be almost as futile as to attempt to remove the blemishes (of which one is aware) in one's early poems. The most remarkable appreciation of Chapman in my time (works of scholarship apart) is to be found in *The Lion and the Fox* by Wyndham Lewis.

I have included one essay, that on John Marston, which was written just too late for inclusion in *Elizabethan Essays*. I have dedicated the present book to the friend and publisher who introduced *Selected Essays* to the American reader in 1932; but I should like to express a debt of gratitude also to the late Charles Whibley, who commissioned *Seneca in Elizabethan Translation* as an introduction in the Tudor Translation Series; and to Sir Bruce Lyttelton Richmond, at whose behest, when he was editor of *The Times Literary Supplement*, I wrote most of the essays on individual dramatists.

                                                    T.S.E.

December 1955.

CONTENTS

CONTENTS

ESSAYS ON ELIZABETHAN DRAMA

Seneca in Elizabethan Translation

No author exercised a wider or deeper influence upon the Elizabethan mind or upon the Elizabethan form of tragedy than did Seneca. To present the Elizabethan translations of the tragedies in their proper setting, it is necessary to deal with three problems which at first may appear to be but slightly connected: (1) the character, virtues, and vices of the Latin tragedies themselves; (2) the directions in which these tragedies influenced our Elizabethan drama; (3) the history of these translations, the part they played in extending the influence of Seneca, and their actual merit as translation and as poetry. There are here several questions which, with the greater number of important Tudor translations, do not arise. Most of the better-known translations are of authors whose intrinsic merit is unquestioned, and the translations derive some of their prestige from the merit and fame of the author translated; and most of the better-known prose translations have an easy beauty of style which arrests even the least prepared reader. But with the Elizabethan translations of the *Tenne Tragedies* (for they are by several hands) we are concerned first of all with a Latin poet whose reputation would deter any reader but the most curious; with translations of unequal merit, because by different scholars; and with translation into a metre—the "fourteener" —which is superficially a mere archaism, and which repels readers who have not the patience to accustom their ears and nerves to its beat. The translations have, as I hope to show, considerable poetic charm and quite adequate accuracy, with occasional flashes of real beauty; their literary value remains greater than that of any later translations of Seneca's tragedies that I have examined, either in English or French. But the appreciation of the literary value of these translations is inseparably engaged with the appreciation of the original and of its historical importance; so that although at first sight a consideration of the historical problems may appear irrelevant, it should in the end enhance our enjoyment of the translations as literature.

I

In the Renaissance, no Latin author was more highly esteemed than Seneca; in modern times, few Latin authors have been more consistently damned. The prose Seneca, the "Seneca morale" of Dante, still enjoys a measure of tepid praise, though he has no influence; but the poet and tragedian receives from the historians and critics of Latin literature the most universal reprobation. Latin literature provides poets for several tastes, but there is no taste

for Seneca. Mackail, for instance, whose taste in
Latin literature is almost catholic, dismisses Seneca
with half a page of his *Short History of Latin Literature,* and a few of the usual adjectives such as
rhetorical. Professor Mackail is inclined by his
training to enjoy the purer and more classical
authors, and is inclined by his temperament to enjoy
the most romantic: like Shenstone or some other
eighteenth-century poets, Seneca falls between.
Nisard, in his *Poètes Latins de la décadence,* devotes
many pages and much patience to the difference of
conditions which produced great tragedy in Athens,
and only rhetorical declamation in Rome. Butler,
after a more detailed and more tolerant examination
from a more literary point of view (*Post-Augustan
Poetry*), commits himself to the damaging statement
that "to Seneca more than to any other man is due
the excessive predominance of declamatory rhetoric,
which has characterised the drama throughout
Western Europe from the Renaissance down to the
latter half of the nineteenth century." The most
recent critic, Mr. F. L. Lucas (*Seneca and Elizabethan Tragedy*), admits "the exasperatingly false
rhetoric of the Senecan stage, with its far-fetched
and frigid epigrams." Yet this is a dramatist whom
Scaliger preferred to Euripides, and whom the
whole of Europe in the Renaissance delighted to
honour. It is obviously a task of some difficulty to
disentangle him from his reputation.

We must admit, first, that the tragedies of Seneca
deserve the censure that has been directed upon
them. On the other hand, it may be true—I think it

is true—that the critics, especially the English critics,
have been often biased by Seneca's real and supposed
bad influence upon the Renaissance, that they have
included the demerits of his admirers in his own
faults. But before we proceed to what redemption of
his fame is possible, it is expedient to resume those
universally admitted strictures and limitations which
have become commonplaces of Senecan criticism.
First, it is pretty generally agreed that the plays of
Seneca were composed, not for stage performance,
but for private declamation.[1] This theory attenuates
the supposed "horrors" of the tragedies, many of
which could hardly have been represented on a stage,
even with the most ingenious machinery, without
being merely ridiculous; the Renaissance assumption
to the contrary gave licence to a taste which would
probably have been indulged even without Seneca's
authority. And if the plays were written to be
declaimed, probably by a single speaker ("elocu-
tionist" is really the word), we can account for other
singularities. I say "account for," I do not say without
qualification that this peculiar form was the "cause";
for the ultimate cause was probably the same Latin
temper which made such an unacted drama possible.
The cause lies in the Latin sensibility which is
expressed by the Latin language. But if we imagine
this unacted drama, we see at once that it is at one
remove from reality, compared with the Greek.
Behind the dialogue of Greek drama we are always

[1] I must admit, however, that this view has recently been
contested with great force by Léon Herrmann: *Le Théâtre de
Sénèque* (Paris, 1924). See p. 195 of that book.

conscious of a concrete visual actuality, and behind that of a specific emotional actuality. Behind the drama of words is the drama of action, the timbre of voice and voice, the uplifted hand or tense muscle, and the particular emotion. The spoken play, the words which we read, are symbols, a shorthand, and often, as in the best of Shakespeare, a very abbreviated shorthand indeed, for the acted and felt play, which is always the real thing. The phrase, beautiful as it may be, stands for a greater beauty still. This is merely a particular case of the amazing unity of Greek, the unity of concrete and abstract in philosophy, the unity of thought and feeling, action and speculation, in life. In the plays of Seneca, the drama is all in the word, and the word has no further reality behind it. His characters all seem to speak with the same voice, and at the top of it; they recite in turn.

I do not mean to suggest that the method of delivery of a play of Seneca was essentially different from that of Greek tragedy. It was probably nearer to the declamation of Greek tragedy than was the delivery of Latin comedy. The latter was acted by professional actors. I imagine that Seneca's plays were declaimed by himself and other amateurs, and it is likely that the Athenian tragedies were performed by amateurs. I mean that the beauty of phrase in Greek tragedy is the shadow of a greater beauty—the beauty of thought and emotion. In the tragedies of Seneca the centre of value is shifted from what the personage says to the way in which he says it. Very often the value comes near to being mere

smartness. Nevertheless, we must remember that
"verbal" beauty is still a kind of beauty.

The plays are admirably adapted for declamation
before an imperial highbrow audience of crude
sensibility but considerable sophistication in the
ingenuities of language. They would have been as
unactable on the Greek stage as they are on the
English. Superficially neat and trim, they are, for
the stage, models of formlessness. The Athenians
were accustomed to long speeches from Messengers,
speeches which embarrass both the modern actor and
the modern audience; this was a convention with
practical advantages; their other long speeches
usually have some dramatic point, some place in the
whole scheme of the play. But the characters in a
play of Seneca behave more like members of a
minstrel troupe sitting in a semicircle, rising in turn
each to do his "number," or varying their recitations
by a song or a little back-chat. I do not suppose that
a Greek audience would have sat through the first
three hundred lines of the *Hercules Furens*. Only at
the 523rd line does Amphitryon detect the sound of
Hercules' tread, ascending from Hell, at which inop-
portune moment the chorus interrupt for two or
three pages. When Hercules finally appears, he seems
to be leading Cerberus, who presently evaporates,
for he is not on the stage a few minutes later. After
Amphitryon has in a rather roundabout way, but
more briefly than might have been expected, explained to Hercules the pressing danger to his family
and country, Hercules makes off to kill Lycus. While
Hercules is thus engaged in a duel on the result of

which everybody's life depends, the family sit down calmly and listen to a long description by Theseus of the Tartarean regions. This account is not a straight monologue, as Amphitryon from time to time puts leading questions about the fauna, and the administration and system of justice, of the world below. Meanwhile, Hercules has (contrary to the usual belief that Seneca murders all his victims in full view of the audience) despatched Lycus off-stage. At the end of the play, when Juno has stricken Hercules with madness, it is not at all clear whether he destroys his family on-stage or off. The slaughter is accompanied by a running commentary by Amphitryon, whose business it is to tell the audience what is going forward. If the children are slain in sight of the audience, this commentary is super-fluous. Amphitryon also reports the collapse of Hercules; but presently Hercules comes to, certainly on-stage, and spies his dead wife and children. The whole situation is inconceivable unless we assume the play to have been composed solely for recitation; like other of Seneca's plays, it is full of statements useful only to an audience which sees nothing. Seneca's plays might, in fact, be practical models for the modern "broadcasted drama."

We need not look too closely into the conditions of the age which produced no genuine drama, but which allowed this curious freak of non-theatrical drama. The theatre is a gift which has not been vouchsafed to every race, even of the highest culture. It has been given to the Hindus, the Japanese, the Greeks; the English, the French, and the Spanish, at moments; in less measure to the Teutons and Scandinavians. It was not given to the Romans, or generously to their successors the Italians. The Romans had some success in low comedy, itself an adaptation of Greek models, but their instinct turned to shows and circuses, as does that of the later race which created the Commedia dell' Arte, which still provides the best puppet shows, and which gives a home to Mr. Gordon Craig. No cause can be assigned, for every cause demands a further cause. It is handy to speak of "the genius of the language," and we shall continue to do so, but why did the language adopt that particular genius? At any rate, we should discourage any criticism which, in accounting for the defects and faults of the plays of Seneca, made much of the "decadence" of the age of Nero. In the verse, yes, Seneca is unquestionably "silver age," or more exactly he is not a poet of the *first* rank in Latin, he is far inferior to Virgil; but for tragic drama, it would be a gross error to suppose that an earlier and more heroic age of Rome could have produced anything better. Many of the faults of Seneca which appear "decadent" are, after all, merely Roman and (in the narrower sense) Latin.

It is so with the characterization. The characters of Seneca's plays have no subtlety and no "private life." But it would be an error to imagine that they are merely cruder and coarser versions of the Greek originals. They belong to a different race. Their crudity is that which was of the Roman, as compared with the Greek, in real life. The Roman was much

the simpler creature. At best, his training was that
of devotion to the State, his virtues were public
virtues. The Greek knew well enough the idea of the
State, but he had also a strong traditional morality
which constituted, so to speak, a direct relation
between him and the gods, without the mediation of
the State, and he had furthermore a sceptical and
heterodox intelligence. Hence the greater efficiency
of the Roman, and the greater interest of the Greek.
Hence the difference between Greek Stoicism and
Roman Stoicism—the latter being the form through
which Stoicism influenced later Europe. We must
think of the characters of Seneca as offspring of
Rome, more than we think of them as offspring of
their age.

The drama of Antigone—which Seneca did not
attempt—could hardly have been transposed for
Roman sentiment. In the drama of Seneca there are no
conflicts, except the conflict of passion, temper, or
appetite with the external duties. The literary consequence, therefore, is the tendency which persists in
modern Italy; the tendency to "rhetoric"; and which,
on such a large scale, may be attributed to a development of language exceeding the development of
sensibility of the people. If you compare Catullus
with Sappho, or Cicero with Demosthenes, or Thucy-
dides with a Latin historian, you find that the genius
is the genius of a different language, and what is
lost is a gift of sensibility. So with Seneca and the
Greek dramatists. Hence we should think of the long
ranting speeches of Seneca, the beautiful but ir-

relevant descriptions, the smart stichomythia, rather
as peculiarities of Latin than as the bad taste of the
dramatist.

The congeniality of Stoicism to the Roman mind
is no part of my duty to analyse; and it would be
futile to attempt to decide what, in the dialogue and
characterization of Seneca's plays, is due to Stoicism,
what due to the Roman mind, and what due to the
peculiar form which Seneca elected. What is certain
is the existence of a large element of Stoicism in the
plays, enough to justify the belief that the plays and
the prose are by the hand of the same Seneca. In the
plays, indeed, the Stoicism is present in a form more
quickly to catch the fancy of the Renaissance than
in the prose epistles and essays. Half of the commonplaces of the Elizabethans—and the more common-
place half—are of Senecan origin. This ethic of
sententious maxims was, as we shall see, much more
sympathetic to the temper of the Renaissance than
would have been the morals of the elder Greek
dramatists; the Renaissance itself was much more
Latin than Greek. In the Greek tragedy, as Nisard
and others have pointed out, the moralising is not
the expression of a conscious "system" of philosophy;
the Greek dramatists moralise only because morals
are woven through and through the texture of
their tragic idea. Their morals are a matter of feeling
trained for generations, they are hereditary and
religious, just as their dramatic forms themselves are
the development of their early liturgies. Their ethics
of thought are one with their ethics of behaviour.
As the dramatic form of Seneca is no growth, but

a construction, so is his moral philosophy and that of Roman Stoicism in general. Whether the Roman scepticism was, as Nisard suggests, the result of a too rapid and great expansion and mixture of races cancelling each other's beliefs, rather than the product of a lively inquiring intelligence, the "beliefs" of Stoicism are a consequence of scepticism; and the ethic of Seneca's plays is that of an age which supplied the lack of moral habits by a system of moral attitudes and poses. To this the natural public temper of Rome contributed. The ethic of Seneca is a matter of postures. The posture which gives the greatest opportunity for effect, hence for the Senecan morality, is the posture of dying: death gives his characters the opportunity for their most sententious aphorisms—a hint which Elizabethan dramatists were only too ready to follow.

When all reserves have been made, there is still much to be said for Seneca as a dramatist. And I am convinced that the proper approach to his appreciation and enjoyment is not by comparison and contrast—to which, in his case, criticism is violently tempted—but by isolation. I made a careful comparison of the *Medea* and the *Hippolytus* of Seneca—perhaps his two best plays—with the *Medea* of Euripides and the *Phèdre* of Racine respectively; but I do not think that any advantage would be gained by reporting the results of this inquiry, by contrasting either the dramatic structure or the treatment of the title figures. Such comparisons have already been made; they magnify the defects and obscure the merits of the Senecan tragedy. If Seneca

is to be compared, he should rather be compared for
versification, descriptive and narrative power, and
taste, with the earlier Roman poets. The comparison
is fair, though Seneca comes off rather ill. His
prosody is monotonous; in spite of a mastery of
several metres, his choruses fall heavily on the ear.
Sometimes his chorus rhythms seem to hover between
the more flexible measures of his predecessors and
the stiffer but more impressive beat of the mediaeval
hymn.[2] But within the limits of his declamatory
purpose, Seneca obtains, time after time, magnificent
effects. In the verbal *coup de théâtre* no one has
ever excelled him. The final cry of Jason to Medea
departing in her car is unique; I can think of no
other play which reserves such a shock for the last
word:

> *Per alta vada spatia sublimi aethere;*
> *testare nullos esse, qua veheris, deos.*[3]

Again and again the epigrammatic observation on
life or death is put in the most telling way at the
most telling moment. It is not only in his brief

[2] E.g. *O mors amoris una sedamen mali,*
　　　O mors pudoris maximum laesi decus.
　　　　　　　　　(Hippolytus, 1188-89.)
[3] Here the translator seems to me to have hit on the sense:

Bear witnesse, grace of God is none in place of thy repayre.

A modern translator (Professor Miller, editing the Loeb
Translation text) gives *"bear witness, where thou ridest, that
there are no gods."* It seems to me more effective if we take the
meaning to be that there are no gods *where (ever) Medea is,*
instead of a mere outburst of atheism. But the old Farnaby
edition observes *"testimonium contra deorum justitiam, vel
argumento nullos esse in caelo deos."*

ejaculations that Seneca triumphs. The sixteen lines
addressed by the chorus to the dead sons of Hercules
(*Hercules Furens*, I. 1135 ff.), which are exquisitely
rendered by the Elizabethan translator, seem to me
highly pathetic. The descriptive passages are often
of great charm, with phrases which haunt us more
than we should expect. The lines of Hercules,

> *ubi sum? sub ortu solis, an sub cardine*
> *glacialis ursae?*

must have lain long in the memory of Chapman
before they came out in *Bussy d' Ambois* as

> *fly where men feel*
> *The cunning axle-tree, or those that suffer*
> *Under the chariot of the snowy Bear.*

Though Seneca is long-winded, he is not diffuse; he
is capable of great concision; there is even a monotony of forcefulness; but many of his short phrases
have for us as much oratorical impressiveness as they
had for the Elizabethans. As (to take an unworn
example) the bitter words of Hecuba as the Greeks
depart:

> *concidit virgo ac puer;*
> *bellum peractum est.*

Even the most sententious sayings of stoical common-
place preserve their solemnity in that Latin language
which carries such thoughts more grandly than could
any other:

> *Fatis agimur; cedite fatis.*
> *non sollicitae possunt curae*

> *mutare rati stamina fusi.*
> *quidquid patimur mortale genus,*
> *quidquid facimus venit ex alto,*
> *servatque suae decreta colus*
> *Lachesis nulla revoluta manu.*
> *omnia secto tramite vadunt*
> *primusque dies dedit extremum.*
>
> (*Oedipus*, 980 ff.)

But to quote Seneca is not criticism; it is merely to offer baits to a possible reader; it would indeed be bad criticism if we left the impression that these and such as these are moments in which Seneca excels himself, and which he could not sustain. An essential point to make about Seneca is the consistency of his writing, its maintenance on one level, below which he seldom falls and above which he never mounts. Seneca is not one of those poets who are to be remembered because they now and then rise to the tone and the vocabulary of greater poets. Seneca is wholly himself; what he attempted he executed, he created his own genre. And this leads us to a consideration which we must keep in mind in considering his later influence: whether we can treat him seriously as a *dramatist*. Critics are inclined to treat his drama as a bastard form. But this is an error which critics of the drama are in general apt to make; the forms of drama are so various that few critics are able to hold more than one or two in mind in pronouncing judgment of "dramatic" and "undramatic." What is "dramatic"? If one were saturated in the Japanese Noh, in Bhasa and

Kalidasa, in Aeschylus, Sophocles and Euripides, Aristophanes and Menander, in the popular medi-aeval plays of Europe, in Lope de Vega and Calderon, as well as the great English and French drama, and if one were (which is impossible) equally sensitive to them all, would one not hesitate to decide that one form is more dramatic than another? And Seneca's is definitely a "form." It does not fall within either of the categories of the defectively dramatic. There are the "closet dramas" which are mostly simply inferior dramas: the plays of Tennyson, Browning, and Swinburne. (Whether a writer expected his play to be played or not is irrelevant, the point is whether it is playable.) And there is another, more interesting type, where the writer is trying to do something more or something different from what the stage can do, but yet with an implication of performance, where there is a mixture of dramatic and extra-dramatic elements. This is a modern and sophisticated form: it contains *The Dynasts*, Goethe's *Faust,* and possibly (not having seen it played I cannot speak with confidence) *Peer Gynt.* Seneca's plays do not belong to either of these types. If, as I believe, they are intended for *recitation,* they have a form of their own; and I believe that they were intended for recitation because they are perfectly adapted for recitation—they are better recited than read. And I have no doubt—though there is no external evidence—that Seneca must have had considerable practice himself in reciting the plays. He would have been, therefore, a playwright of as practical experience as Shakespeare or Molière. His form is a practical form; it is even, I suggest, a form which might be interesting to attempt in our own time, when the revival of the theatre is obstructed by some of the difficulties which made the stage an impossibility in the age of Seneca.

What lessons the Elizabethans learnt from Seneca, and whether they were the same as those which we might learn ourselves, is the next subject to consider. But whether they profited by the study, or whether they admired him and pillaged him to their own detriment, we must remember that we cannot justly estimate his influence unless we form our own opinion of Seneca first, without being influenced by his influence.

II

The influence of Seneca upon Elizabethan drama has received much more attention from scholars than from literary critics. The historical treatment has been very thorough. The admirable edition of the works of Sir William Alexander, Earl of Stirling, by Kastner and Charlton (Manchester University Press, vol. i, 1921), has a full account of this influence both direct and through Italy and France; in this introduction also will be found the best bibliography of the subject. Dr. F. S. Boas, especially in his edition of Kyd's Plays, has treated the matter at length. Professor J. W. Cunliffe's *Influence of Seneca on Elizabethan Tragedy* (1893) remains, within its limits, the most useful of all books, and Mr. Cunliffe has handled the question in a more general way in his *Early English Classical Tragedies.* Indirect Senecan influences have also been studied in detail, as in Professor A. M. Witherspoon's *Influence of Robert Garnier on Elizabethan Drama.* And work which is now being done on the earlier drama (see Dr. A. W. Reed's recent *Early Tudor Drama,* 1926) will enable us to understand better the junction of the Senecan influence with the native tradition. It is not fitting that a literary critic should retrace all this labour of scholarship, where either his dissent or his approval would be an impertinence; but we may benefit by this scholarship to draw certain general conclusions.

The plays of Seneca exerted their influence in several ways and to several results. The results are of three main types: (1) the popular Elizabethan tragedy; (2) the "Senecal" drama, pseudo-classical, composed by and for a small and select body of persons not closely in touch or in sympathy with the popular drama of the day, and composed largely in protest against the defects and monstrosities of that drama; (3) the two Roman tragedies of Ben Jonson, which appear to belong between the two opposed classes, to constitute an attempt, by an active practising playwright, to improve the form of popular drama by the example of Seneca; not by slavish imitation but by adaptation, to make of popular drama a finished work of art. As for the ways in which Seneca influenced the Elizabethans, it must be remembered that these were never simple, and became more complicated. The Italian and the French drama of the day was already penetrated by

Seneca. Seneca was a regular part of the school curriculum, while Greek drama was unknown to all but a few great scholars. Every schoolboy with a smattering of Latin had a verse or two of Seneca in his memory; probably a good part of the audiences could recognise the origin of the occasional bits of Seneca which are quoted in Latin in some of the popular plays (*e.g.* several times by Marston). And by the time that *The Spanish Tragedy* and the old *Hamlet* had made their success, the English playwright was under the influence of Seneca by being under the influence of his own predecessors. Here the influence of Kyd is of the greatest importance: if Senecan Kyd had such a vogue, that was surely the path to facile success for any hard-working and underpaid writer.

All that I wish to do is to consider certain misconceptions of the Senecan influence, which I believe are still current in our opinions of Elizabethan drama, although they do not appear in works of scholarship. For such a purpose the contemporary translations possess a particular value: whether they greatly affected the conception of Seneca, or greatly extended his influence, they give a reflection of the appearance of Seneca to the Englishman of the time. I do not suggest that the influence of Seneca has been exaggerated or diminished in modern criticism; but I believe that too much importance has been attached to his influence in some directions, and too little to his influence in others. There is one point on which every one is agreed, and hardly more than one: the five-act division of the modern

European play is due to Seneca. What I chiefly wish
to consider are, first, his responsibility for what has
been called since Symonds' day the Tragedy of
Blood—how far Seneca is the author of the horrors
which disfigure Elizabethan drama; second, his responsibility for *bombast* in Elizabethan diction; and
third, his influence upon the *thought,* or what passes
for thought, in the drama of Shakespeare and his contemporaries. It is the first which I think has been
overestimated, the second misconstrued, the third
undervalued.

Certainly, among all national dramas, the Elizabethan tragedies are remarkable for the extent to
which they employ the horrible and revolting. It
is true that but for this taste and practice we should
never have had *King Lear* or *The Duchess of Malfy;*
so impossible is it to isolate the vices from the
virtues, the failures from the masterpieces of Elizabethan tragedy. We cannot reprehend a custom but
for which one great experiment of the human spirit
must have been left unmade, even if we cannot
like it; nor can we wholly deplore anything which
brings with it some information about the soul. And
even leaving Shakespeare apart, the genius of no other
race could have manipulated the tragedy of horror
into the magnificent farce of Marlowe, or the magnificent nightmare of Webster. We must therefore
reserve two measures of comparison: one, that between the baser tragedy of the time and the best
tragedy of the time, the other (which is perhaps a
moral measure, the application of which would lead
us too far for the present discussion) between the

tragedy of the time as a whole and another tragedy of horror—we think of Dante's Ugolino and the Oedipus of Sophocles—in which, in the end, the mind seems to triumph. Here, the question of Seneca's influence is capital. If the taste for horror was a result of being trained on Seneca, then it has neither justification nor interest; if it was something inherent in the people and in the age, and Seneca merely the excuse and precedent, then it is a phenomenon of interest. Even to speak of Seneca as offering a precedent and excuse is probably to falsify; for it implies that the Elizabethans would otherwise have been a little uneasy in conscience at indulging such taste—which is ridiculous to suppose. They merely assumed that Seneca's taste was like their own—which is not *wholly* untrue; and that Seneca represented the whole of classical antiquity—which is quite false. Where Seneca took part is in affecting the type of plot; he supported one tendency against another. But for Seneca, we might have had more plays in *The Yorkshire Tragedy* mould; that is to say, the equivalent of the *News of the World* murder report; Seneca, and particularly the Italianised Seneca, encouraged the taste for the foreign, remote, or exotic. No doubt *The Jew of Malta* or *Titus Andronicus* would have made the living Seneca shudder with genuine aesthetic horror; but his influence helped to recommend work with which he had little in common.

When we examine the plays of Seneca, the actual horrors are not so heinous or so many as are supposed. The most unpleasantly sanguinary is the

Thyestes, a subject which, so far as I know, was not attempted by a Greek dramatist. Even here, if the view that the tragedies were intended only for recitation is true, the cultivated Roman audience were listening to a story which was part of their Hellenic culture, and which is in fact a common property of folklore. The story was sanctified by time. The plots of Elizabethan tragedy were, so far as the audience were concerned, novelties. This plot of *Thyestes* is not employed by any Elizabethan, but the play has undoubtedly more in common with the Tragedy of Blood, especially in its early form, than any other of Seneca's. It has a particularly tedious Ghost. It has, more emphatically than any other, the motive of Revenge, unregulated by any divine control or justice. Yet even in the *Thyestes* the performance of the horrors is managed with conventional tact; the only visible horror is the perhaps unavoidable presentation of the evidence—the children's heads in a dish.

The most significant popular play under Senecan influence is of course *The Spanish Tragedy,* and the further responsibility of Kyd for the translation of the pseudo-Senecan *Cornelia* of Garnier has marked him as the disciple of Seneca. But in *The Spanish Tragedy* there is another element, not always sufficiently distinguished from the Senecan, which (though it may have relations among the Italian Renaissance progeny of Seneca) allies it to something more indigenous. The Senecan apparatus, it is true, is impressive. The Ghost, and Revenge, who replace the Tantalus and the Fury of the *Thyestes,* use all

the infernal allusions—Acheron, Charon, and the
rest—so dear to Seneca. Temporary insanity is an
expedient well known to Seneca. But in the type of
plot there is nothing classical or pseudoclassical at
all. "Plot" in the sense in which we find plot in *The
Spanish Tragedy* does not exist for Seneca. He took a
story perfectly well known to everybody, and interested his auditors entirely by his embellishments of
description and narrative and by smartness and pun-
gency of dialogue; suspense and surprise attached
solely to verbal effects. *The Spanish Tragedy*, like
the series of Hamlet plays, including Shakespeare's,
has an affinity to our contemporary detective drama.[4]
The plot of Hieronymo to compass his revenge by
the play allies it with a small but interesting class of
drama which certainly owes nothing essential to
Seneca: that which includes *Arden of Feversham*[5]
and *The Yorkshire Tragedy*. These two remarkable
plays are both based on contemporary or recent
crimes committed in England. Unless it be the hint
of divine retribution in the epilogue to *Arden*, there
is no token of foreign or classical influence in these
two plays. Yet they are bloody enough. The husband
in *The Yorkshire Tragedy* kills his two young sons,
throws the servant downstairs and breaks her neck,

[4] I suggest also that besides *Hamlet*, *Macbeth* and to some
extent *Othello* among Shakespeare's major tragedies have this
"thriller" interest, whilst it is not introduced into *King Lear*,
Antony and Cleopatra, or *Coriolanus*. It is present in *Oedipus
Tyrannus*.

[5] I dissent from Dr. Boas, and agree with that body of
opinion which attributes *Arden* to Kyd, *e.g.* Fleay, Robertson,
Crawford, Dugdale Sykes, Oliphant.

and nearly succeeds in killing his wife. In *Arden of Feversham* the wife and her conspirators stab the husband to death upon the stage—the rest of the play being occupied by a primitive but effective police inquiry. It is only surprising that there are not more examples of this type of play, since there is evidence of as lively a public interest in police court horrors as there is today. One of the pieces of evidence is associated with Kyd; it is a curious little account of a poisoning case, *The Murder of John Brewen*. (A little later, Dekker was to supply the deficiency of penny journalism with his Plague Pamphlets.) In Kyd, whether *Arden* be by him or by an imitator, we find the union of Senecan with native elements, to the advantage of both. For the Senecan influence is felt in the structure of the play—the structure of *The Spanish Tragedy* is more dramatic than that of *Arden* or *The Yorkshire Tragedy;* whilst the material of *The Spanish Tragedy,* like that of the other two plays, is quite different from the Senecan material, and much more satisfying to an unlettered audience.

The worst that can be urged against Seneca, in the matter of responsibility for what is disgusting in Elizabethan drama, is that he may have provided the dramatist with a pretext or justification for horrors which were not Senecan at all, for which there was certainly a taste, and the taste for which would certainly have been gratified at that time whether Seneca had ever written or not. Against my use of *The Yorkshire Tragedy,* it may be said that this play (the crime in question was committed only in 1603) and *Arden* also were written after the success of *The Spanish Tragedy,* and that the taste for horrors developed only after it had received Senecan licence. I cannot *prove* the contrary. But it must be admitted that the greater number of the horrors are such as Seneca himself would not have tolerated. In one of the worst offenders—indeed one of the stupidest and most uninspired plays ever written, a play in which it is incredible that Shakespeare had any hand at all, a play in which the best passages would be too highly honoured by the signature of Peele—in *Titus Andronicus*[6]—there is nothing really Senecan at all. There is a wantonness, an irrelevance, about the crimes of which Seneca would never have been guilty. Seneca's Oedipus has the traditional justification for blinding himself; and the blinding itself is far less offensive than that in *Lear*. In *Titus,* the hero cuts off his own hand in view of the audience, who can also testify to the mutilation of the hands and the tongue of Lavinia. In *The Spanish Tragedy,* Hieronymo bites off his own tongue. There is nothing like this in Seneca.

But if this is very unlike Seneca, it is very like the contemporary drama of Italy. Nothing could better illustrate the accidental character of literary "influence"—accidental, that is, with reference to the work exercising the influence—than the difference between Senecan drama in Italy and in France. The French drama is from the beginning restrained and decorous; to the French drama, especially to Garnier,

[6] See J. M. Robertson: *An Introduction to the Study of the Shakespeare Canon.*

the Senecan drama of Greville, Daniel, and Alexander is allied. The Italian is bloodthirsty in the extreme. Kyd knew both; but it was to the Italian that he and Peele yielded themselves with sympathetic delight. We must remember, too, that Italy had developed stagecraft and stage machinery to the highest point—for the most sumptuous masques in England, Italian managers, engineers and artists were brought over; that the plastic arts were much more important in Italy than elsewhere, and that consequently the spectacular and sensational elements of drama were insisted upon; that Italian civilisation had, in short, everything to dazzle the imagination of unsophisticated northerners emerging into a period of prosperity and luxury. I have no first-hand acquaintance with Italian plays of this epoch; it is a library which few readers would penetrate in pursuit of pleasure; but its character and influence in England are well attested. It is possible to say that Seneca hardly influenced this Italian drama at all; he was made use of by it and adopted into it; and for Kyd and Peele he was thoroughly Italianised.

The Tragedy of Blood is very little Senecan, in short, though it made much use of Senecan machinery; it is very largely Italian; and it added an ingenuity of plot which is native.

If we wished to find the reason for the sanguinary character of much Elizabethan drama—which persists to its end—we should have to allow ourselves some daring generalizations concerning the temper of the epoch. When we consider it, and reflect how much more refined, how much more *classical* in the profounder sense, is that earlier popular drama which reached its highest point in *Everyman,* I cannot but think that the change is due to some fundamental release of restraint. The tastes gratified are always latent: they were then gratified by the drama, as they are now gratified by crime reports in the daily press. It is no more reasonable to make Seneca responsible for this aspect of Elizabethan drama than it is to connect Aeschylus or Sophocles with *Jude the Obscure.* I am not sure that the latter association has not been made, though no one supposes that Hardy prepared himself by close application to the study of Greek drama.

It is pertinent to inquire, in this context, what was the influence of Seneca, in the way of horrors, upon the small body of "Senecal" dramatists who professionally imitated him. But this collation is relevant also to the question of Seneca's influence upon language; so that before making the comparison we may consider this latter question next. Here, the great influence of Seneca is unquestionable. Quotation after quotation, parallel after parallel, may be adduced; the most conspicuous are given in Cunliffe's *Influence of Seneca,* others in Lucas's *Seneca and Elizabethan Tragedy.* So great is this influence that we can say neither that it was good nor that it was bad; for we cannot imagine what Elizabethan dramatic verse would have been without it. The direct influence is restricted to the group of Marlowe and to Marston; Jonson and Chapman are, each in his own way, more sophisticated and independent; the later or Jacobean dramatists, Middleton, Webster,

Tourneur, Ford, Beaumont and Fletcher, found their language upon their own predecessors, and chiefly upon Shakespeare. But none of these authors hesitated to draw upon Seneca when occasion served, and Chapman owes much, both good and bad, of his dramatic style to his admiration for Seneca. No better examples can be found, however, of plays which, while not Senecan in form, are yet deeply influenced by Seneca in language, than the *True Tragedy of Richard Duke of York,* and the Shakespearean *Richard II* and *Richard III.* These, with the work of Kyd and that of Marlowe and of Peele, and several of the plays included in the Shakespeare Apocrypha, have a great deal in common.

The precise pilferings and paraphrases have been thoroughly catalogued by the scholars I have mentioned, and others; hardly a dramatist, between Kyd and Massinger, is not many times indebted to Seneca. Instead of repeating this labour, I prefer to call attention to his universal influence. Not only the evolution of the dramatic structure, but the evolution of the blank verse cadence, took place under the shadow of Seneca; it is hardly too much to say that Shakespeare could not have formed the verse instrument which he left to his successors, Webster, Massinger, Tourneur, Ford, and Fletcher, unless he had received an instrument already highly developed by the genius of Marlowe and the influence of Seneca. Blank verse before 1600, or thereabouts, is a crude form of music compared to blank verse after that date; but its progress in fifteen years had been astonishing. In the first place, I believe that the establishment of blank verse as the vehicle of drama, instead of the old fourteener, or the heroic couplet, or (what might have happened) a particular form of prose rhythm, received considerable support from its being obviously the nearest equivalent to the solemnity and weight of the Senecan iambic. A comparison of the trotting metre of our translations with Surrey's translation of Virgil will show, I think, that while the former has undeniable poetic charms of its own, the latter would reveal more resources to the ear of the dramatist. The pre-Marlowe versification is competent, but extremely monotonous; it is literally a *monotone,* containing none of the musical counterrhythms which Marlowe introduced, nor the rhythms of individual speech which were later added.

> *When this eternal substance of my soul*
> *Did live imprison'd in my wanton flesh,*
> *Each in their function serving other's need,*
> *I was a courtier in the Spanish court:*
>> (Prologue, *Spanish Tragedy,* xxx.)

But to illustrate the early use of this metre under Senecan influence, a worse play serves our purpose better; the Senecan content justifies our quoting at some length from *Locrine,* an early play[7] of no merit whatever. Here is the Revival of Learning in the brain of a fourth-rate playwright:

---

[7] Usually attributed to Greene, and dated about 1585 (see Brooke, *Shakespeare Apocrypha*). Neither authorship nor date is important for my purpose: the play was obviously written by some one who had not yet experienced the influence of Marlowe.

HUMBER.

　　Where may I find some desert wilderness,
　　Where I may breathe out curses as I would,
　　And scare the earth with my condemning voice;
　　Where every echo's repercussion
　　May help me to bewail mine overthrow,
　　And aid me in my sorrowful laments?
　　Where may I find some hollow uncouth rock,
　　Where I may damn, condemn, and ban my fill
　　The heavens, the hell, the earth, the air, the fire,
　　And utter curses to the concave sky,
　　Which may infect the airy regions,
　　And light upon the Brittain Locrine's head?
　　You ugly sprites that in Cocytus mourn,
　　And gnash your teeth with dolorous laments:
　　You fearful dogs that in black Lethe howl,
　　And scare the ghosts with your wide open throats:
　　You ugly ghosts that, flying from these dogs,
　　Do plunge yourselves in Puryflegiton:
　　Come, all of you, and with your shriking notes
　　Accompany the Brittain's conquering host.
　　Come, fierce Erynnys, horrible with snakes;
　　Come, ugly Furies, armed with your whips;
　　You threefold judges of black Tartarus,
　　And all the army of you hellish fiends,
　　With new-found torments rack proud Locrine's
　　　　　bones!
　　O gods, and stars! damned be the gods and stars
　　That did not drown me in fair Thetis' plains!
　　Curst be the sea, that with outrageous waves,
　　With surging billows did not rive my ships

Against the rocks of high Cerannia,
Or swallow me into her wat'ry gulf!
Would God we had arriv'd upon the shore
Where Polyphemus and the Cyclops dwell,
Or where the bloody Anthropophagi
With greedy jawes devours the wand'ring wights!

Enter the ghost of ALBANACT

But why comes Albanact's bloody ghost,
To bring a corsive to our miseries?
Is 't not enough to suffer shameful flight,
But we must be tormented now with ghosts,
With apparitions fearful to behold?

GHOST.

Revenge! revenge for blood!

HUMBER.

So nought will satisfy your wand'ring ghost
But dire revenge, nothing but Humber's fall,
Because he conquered you in Albany.
Now, by my soul, Humber would be condemned
To Tantal's hunger or Ixion's wheel,
Or to the vulture of Prometheus,
Rather than that this murder were undone.
When as I die I'll drag thy cursed ghost
Through all the rivers of foul Erebus,
Through burning sulphur of the Limbo-lake,
To allay the burning fury of that heat
That rageth in mine everlasting soul.

GHOST.

Vindicta, vindicta.   [Exeunt.

This is the proper Ercles bombast, ridiculed by Shakespeare, Jonson, and Nashe. From this, even to *Tamburlaine,* is a long way; it is too absurdly distorted to serve even as a burlesque of Seneca; but the metre has something Senecan about it. From such verse there is a long distance to the melodies of

Now comes my lover tripping like a roe,
And brings my longings tangled in her hair.

or

Welcome, my son: who are the violets now
That strew the green lap of the new-come spring?

or

But look, the morn, in russet mantle clad,
Walks o'er the dew of yon high eastern hill:

that is to say, to the *lyrical* phase of blank verse, before Shakespeare had analysed it into true dramatic differentiation; it belongs to the first or *declamatory* phase. But this declamation is in its impulse, if not in its achievement, Senecan; and progress was made, not by rejection, but by dissociating this type of verse into products with special properties.

The next stage also was reached with the help of a hint from Seneca. Several scholars, Butler in particular, have called attention to a trick of Seneca of repeating one word of a phrase in the next phrase, especially in stichomythia, where the sentence of one speaker is caught up and twisted by the next. This was an effective stage trick, but it is something more; it is the crossing of one rhythm pattern with another.

 —*Sceptrone nostro* famulus *est potior tibi?*
 —*Quot iste* famulus *tradidit* reges *neci.*
 —*Cur ergo* regi *servit et patitur iugum?*
          (*Hercules.*)

Seneca also gets a kind of double pattern by breaking up lines into minimum antiphonal units:

 Rex est timendus.
       Rex meus fuerat pater.
 Non metuis arma?
        Sint licet terra edita.
 Moriere.
    Cupio.
      Profuge.
        Paenituit fugae.
 Medea,
   Fiam.
     Mater es.
       Cui sim vides.
       (*Medea,* 168 ff.)

A man like Marlowe, or even men with less scholarship and less genius for the use of words than he, could hardly have failed to learn something from this. At any rate, I believe that the study of Seneca had its part in the formation of verse like the following:

 —*Wrong not her birth, she is of royal blood.*
 —*To save her life, I'll say she is not so.*
 —*Her life is safest only in her birth.*
 —*And only in that safety died her brothers.*

It is only a step (and a few lines further) to the pun:

Cousins, indeed; and by their uncle cozen'd.

Some of the effects in such plays as *Richard II* and *Richard III* are indeed of pre-Marlowe origin, as:

I had an Edward, till a Richard kill'd him;
I had a Henry, till a Richard kill'd him;
Thou hadst an Edward, till a Richard kill'd him;
Thou hadst a Richard, till a Richard kill'd him.

which is already in even *Locrine*, as:

The boisterous Boreas thundreth forth Revenge,
The stony rocks cry out on sharp revenge,
The thorny bush pronounceth dire revenge,

but in the following lines from Clarence's Dream we see an immense advance over *Locrine* in the use of infernal machinery:

I pass'd, methought, the melancholy flood,
With that grim ferryman which poets write of,
Unto the kingdom of perpetual night.
The first that there did greet my stranger soul,
Was my great father-in-law, renowned Warwick;
Who cried aloud, "What scourge for perjury
Can this dark monarchy afford false Clarence?"[8]

The "kingdom of perpetual night" and the last two lines are a real approximation in English to the

---

[8] I once expressed the opinion that these lines must be by Shakespeare. I am not so confident now. See J. M. Robertson: *The Shakespeare Canon*, Part II.

magnificence of Senecan Latin at its best; they are
far from being a mere burlesque. The best of Seneca
has here been absorbed into English.

In *Richard II*, which is usually dated a little earlier
than *Richard III*, I find such interesting variations of
versification that I am convinced that it is a slightly
later play,[9] or else that there is more of Shakespeare
in it. There is the same play of words:

Give Richard leave to live till Richard die.

A brittle glory shineth in his face;
As brittle as the glory is the face.

but there is less stichomythia, less mere repetition,
and a dexterity in retaining and developing the
same rhythm with greater freedom and less obvious
calculation. (See the long speeches of Richard in
Act III, sc. ii and sc. iii, and compare with the more
carefully balanced verses of Queen Margaret's tirade
in *Richard III*, Act IV, sc. iv.)

When blank verse has reached this point, and
passed into the hands of its greatest master, there is
no need to look for fresh infusions of Seneca. He has
done his work and the one influence on later dramatic blank verse is the influence of Shakespeare.
Not that later dramatists do not make great use of
Seneca's plays. Chapman uses him, and employs the
old machinery; but Seneca's influence on Chapman
was chiefly on Chapman's "thought." Jonson uses

[9] I do not deny that some parts, or some lines, of *Richard
III* are later than *Richard II*. Both plays may have undergone
revision from time to time, and in any case must be dated
near together.

Seneca deliberately; the superb prologues of *Envy* and *Sylla's Ghost* are adaptations of the Senecan ghost-prologue form, not an inheritance from Kyd. Massinger, a most accomplished dramatist and versifier, sometimes falls back most lamentably upon ghosts and spectacles. But the verse is formed, and Seneca no further responsible for its vices or virtues.

Certainly, Elizabethan bombast can be traced to Seneca; Elizabethans themselves ridiculed the Senecan imitation. But if we reflect, not on the more grotesque exaggerations, but on the dramatic poetry of the first half of the period, as a whole, we see that Seneca had as much to do with its merits and its progress as with its faults and its delays. Certainly it is all "rhetorical," but if it had not been rhetorical, would it have been anything? Certainly it is a relief to turn back to the austere, close language of *Everyman,* the simplicity of the mysteries; but if new influences had not entered, old orders decayed, would the language not have left some of its greatest resources unexplored? Without bombast, we should not have had *King Lear.* The art of dramatic language, we must remember, is as near to oratory as to ordinary speech or to other poetry. If the Elizabethans distorted and travestied Seneca in some ways, if they learned from him tricks and devices which they applied with inexpert hands, they also learned from him the essentials of declaimed verse. Their subsequent progress is a process of splitting up the primitive rhetoric, developing out of it subtler poetry and subtler tones of conversation, eventually mingling, as no other school of dramatists has done, the oratorical, the conversational, the elaborate and the simple, the direct and the indirect; so that they were able to write plays which can still be viewed as plays, with any plays, and which can still be read as poetry, with any poetry.

It is improper to pass from the questions of Seneca's influence upon the Tragedy of Blood and upon the language of the Elizabethans without mentioning the group of "Senecal" plays, largely produced under the aegis of the Countess of Pembroke. The history of this type of play belongs rather to the history of scholarship and culture than to the history of the Drama: it begins in a sense with the household of Sir Thomas More, and therefore is doubly allied to the present subject by Jasper Heywood; it is continued in the conversations at Cambridge of Mr. Ascham, Mr. Watson, and Mr. (later Sir John) Cheke. The first to attack openly the common stage was Sir Philip Sidney, whose words are well known:

"Our Tragedies and Comedies (not without cause cried out against), observing rules neither of honest civility nor of skilful Poetry, excepting *Gorboduc* (againe, I say, of those that I have seen), which notwithstanding, as it is full of stately speeches and well sounding Phrases, climbing to the height of Seneca his style, and as full of notable morality, which it doth most delightfully teach, and so obtain the very end of Poesie, yet in troth it is very defectious in the circumstances, which grieveth me, because it might not remain as an exact model of all Tragedies. For it is faulty both in place and time, the two necessary

companions of all corporal actions. . . . But if it be
so in *Gorboduc,* how much more in all the rest,
where you shall have Asia of the one side, and Afric
of the other, and so many other under-kingdoms,
that the Player, when he cometh in, must ever begin
with telling where he is: or else the tale will not be
conceived? Now ye shall have three Ladies walk to
gather flowers, and then we must believe the stage to
be a Garden. By and by, we hear news of shipwrack
in the same place, and then we are to blame if we
accept it not for a Rock."

It was after Sidney's death that his sister, the
Countess of Pembroke, tried to assemble a body of
wits to compose drama in the proper Senecan style,
to make head against the popular melodrama of the
time. Great poetry should be both an art and a
diversion; in a large and cultivated public like the
Athenian it can be both; the shy recluses of Lady
Pembroke's circle were bound to fail. But we must
not draw too sharp a line of separation between the
careful workman who laboured to create a classical
drama in England and the hurried purveyors of
playhouse successes: the two worlds were not without
communication, and the work of the earlier Senecals
was not without fruit.

With the part played by the *Tenne Tragedies* in
this Senecan tradition I shall deal in the next section
of this essay. Here, I wish only to call attention to
certain characteristics of Senecal Tragedy in its final
form, in the work of Greville, Daniel, and Alexander.
I would only remind the reader that these final

Senecal plays were written after any real hope of
altering or reforming the English stage had disap-
peared. In the early Elizabethan years appeared a
succession of tragedies, mostly performed by the Inns
of Court, and therefore not popular productions,
which might in favourable circumstances have led
to a living Senecan drama. Notably, *Gorboduc* (mentioned by Sidney above), *Jocasta,* and *Gismond of
Salerne* (three of the four plays contained in Cunliffe's *Early English Classical Tragedies*). When *The
Spanish Tragedy* appeared (with, as I have suggested,
its particularly non-classical element) these feeble
lights were snuffed out. I pass on to the finished
Senecal product, because I am only concerned to
elicit the effect of Seneca upon his sedulous admirers
and imitators who professed to be, and were, men of
taste and culture.

The Monarchic Tragedies of Alexander, Earl of
Stirling, are the last on our list, composed under the
auspices of the scholarly King James I. They are
poor stuff: I imagine that they are more important
in the history of the Union than in the history of
the Drama, since they represent the choice, by a
Scotsman of accidental eminence, to write verse in
English instead of in Scots. Their faults are the
faults of the other plays of the group; but they have
not the virtues of the others. The two plays of Fulke
Greville, Lord Brooke, the friend and biographer of
Sidney, have some magnificent passages, especially in
the choruses; Greville had a true gift for sententious
declamation. But they have much dullness also; and

they do not imitate Seneca nearly so faithfully as either those of Alexander or those of Daniel. Greville not only cannot stick to one chorus, but will introduce, on one occasion, a chorus of "Bashas or Caddies," and after the next act, a chorus of "Mahometan Priests"; he introduces the still more doubtful practice of supernatural figures, a "dialogue of Good and Evil Spirits," or even a chorus of two allegorical figures, "Time and Eternity" (ending indeed with the fine line spoken by Eternity: *I am the measure of felicity*). The best, the best sustained, the most poetic and the most lyrical, are two tragedies of Samuel Daniel: *Cleopatra* and *Philotas*. They contain many lovely passages, they are readable all through, and they are well built.

Now, in comparison with the supposed influence of Seneca on the barbarity of Elizabethan tragedy, and his supposed bad influence upon the language, what do we find in the plays of those who took him as their model in their attack upon the popular stage, in that attack in which Daniel, in his dedication of *Cleopatra* to the Countess of Pembroke, declared himself the foe of "Gross Barbarism"? Deaths there are, of course, but there is none of these tragedies that is not far more restrained, far more discreet and sober, not only than the Tragedy of Blood, but than Seneca himself. Characters die so decently, so remote from the stage, and the report of their deaths is wrapped up in such long speeches by messengers stuffed with so many moral maxims, that we may read on unaware that any one concerned in the play has died at all. Where the popular playwrights travestied Seneca's melodrama and his fury, the Senecals travesty his reserve and his decorum. And as for the language, that, too, is a different interpretation of Seneca. How vague are our notions of bombast and rhetoric when they must include styles and vocabularies so different as those of Kyd and Daniel! It is by opposite excesses that Senecals and popular dramatists attract the same reproach. The language of Daniel is pure and restrained; the vocabulary choice, the expression clear; there is nothing far-fetched, conceited, or perverse.

CLEOPATRA.

What, hath my face yet power to win a Lover?
Can this torne remnant serve to grace me so,
That it can Caesar's secret plots discover,
What he intends with me and mine to do?
Why then, poor beauty, thou hast done thy last,
And best good service thou could'st do unto me;
For now the time of death reveal'd thou hast,
Which in my life did'st serve but to undo me.

The first two lines are admirable; the rest are good serviceable lines; almost any passage from *Cleopatra* is as good, and some are far better. The whole thing is in excellent taste. Yet we may ponder the fact that it would not have made the slightest difference, to the formation of our Augustan poetry, if Daniel and his friends had never written a line; that Dryden and Pope are nearer allied to—Cowley; and that they owe more to Marlowe than to the purest taste of the sixteenth century. Daniel and Greville are good poets, and there is something to be learned from them; but they, and Sir John Davies who somewhat resembles them, had no influence. The only one of Lady Pembroke's heroes who had influence is Edmund Spenser.

Within the limits of an essay it is impossible to do more than touch on the influence of Seneca upon the "thought" of the Elizabethans, or more exactly, upon their attitude toward life so far as it can be formulated in words. I would only say enough, at this point, to remind the reader that Seneca's influence upon dramatic form, upon versification and language, upon sensibility, and upon thought, must in the end be all estimated together; they cannot be divided. How the influence of Seneca is related, in the Elizabethan mind, with other influences, perhaps those of Montaigne and Machiavelli, I do not know; and I think it is a subject still to be investigated. But the frequency with which a quotation from Seneca, or a thought or figure ultimately derived from Seneca, is employed in Elizabethan plays whenever a moral reflection is required, is too remarkable to be ignored; and when an Elizabethan hero or villian dies, he usually dies in the odour of Seneca. These facts are known to scholars; but if known, they are usually ignored by literary critics. In a comparison of Shakespeare with Dante, for instance, it is assumed than Dante leant upon a system of philosophy which he accepted whole, whereas Shake-

speare created his own: or that Shakespeare had
acquired some extra- or ultra-intellectual knowledge
superior to a philosophy. This occult kind of information is sometimes called "spiritual knowledge"
or "insight." Shakespeare and Dante were both
merely poets (and Shakespeare a dramatist as well);
our estimate of the intellectual material they absorbed does not affect our estimate of their poetry,
either absolutely or relatively to each other. But it
must affect our vision of them and the use we make
of them, the fact that Dante, for instance, had behind him an Aquinas, and Shakespeare behind him
a Seneca. Perhaps it was Shakespeare's special rôle in
history to have effected this peculiar union—perhaps
it is a part of his special eminence to have expressed
an inferior philosophy in the greatest poetry. It is
certainly one cause of the terror and awe with which
he inspires us.

> *Omnia certo tramite vadunt*
> *primusque dies dedit extremum.*
> *non illa deo vertisse licet*
> *quae nexa suis currunt causis.*
> *it cuique ratus prece non ulla*
> *mobilis ordo.*
> *multis ipsum timuisse nocet.*
> *multi ad fatum venere suum*
> *dum fata timent.*

Compare with *Edward III,* Act IV, sc. iv (see Cunliffe, *Influence of Seneca,* p. 87), and with *Measure
for Measure,* Act III, sc. i. And

> *Men must endure*
> *Their going hence, even as their coming hither,*
> *Ripeness is all.*[10]

III

The *Tenne Tragedies* were translated and printed separately over a space of about eight years, with the exception of the *Thebais*, which was translated by Newton in 1581 to complete the work for his edition of the whole. The order and dates of the several translations are of interest. The first and best of the translators was Jasper Heywood:[11] his *Troas* was printed in 1559, his *Thyestes* in 1560, his *Hercules Furens* in 1561. The *Oedipus* by Alexander Nevyle (translated 1560) was printed in 1563. In 1566 appeared the *Octavia* of Nuce, the *Agamemnon*,

[10] Mr. F. L. Lucas, in his *Seneca and Elizabethan Tragedy*, says (p. 122): "But it must be said once for all about the bulk of Shakespeare's supposed borrowings from Seneca, that one grows more and more sceptical." What has been said once for all is not for me to dispute, but I would point out that I am not here concerned with Shakespeare's "borrowings" (where I am inclined to agree) but with Shakespeare as the voice of his time, and this voice in poetry is, in the most serious matters of life and death, most often the voice of Seneca. I subscribe to the observation of Cunliffe (*op. cit.* p. 85): "We have [in *King Lear*] Seneca's hopeless fatalism, not only in the catastrophe, but repeatedly brought forward in the course of the play."

> *As flies to wanton boys are we to the gods;*
> *They kill us for their sport.*

[11] Sometime Fellow of All Souls College, and later an eminent Jesuit; but chiefly remembered as the uncle of John Donne. Much information about Heywood and his family is contained in A. W. Reed's *Early Tudor Drama*.

Medea, and *Hercules Oetaeus* of Studley in 1566,
and the *Hippolytus* of Studley probably in 1567.
About fourteen years then elapsed before Newton
produced his complete edition, and it may be pre-
sumed that he translated the *Thebais* for that
purpose.[12]

It has never been supposed, in spite of the acid
taunt of Nashe, that any of the Elizabethan dramatists owe any great debt to these translations.[13] Most
of the playwrights, as I have intimated before, may
be supposed to have had a smattering of Seneca at
school; two of the popular dramatists who exercised
a decisive influence at an important moment—Kyd
and Peele—were acquainted with several languages,
and therefore themselves subjected to several influences. But if we look at the dates we cannot over-
look the probability that these translations helped to
direct the course of events. They (all but one) appeared between 1559 and 1566. The first plays of
Senecan form which could be called popular were
Sackville and Norton's *Gorboduc,* which appeared
in 1561, Gascoyne's *Jocasta* in 1566, and *Gismond
of Salerne* in 1567. We must also take account, of
course, of the fact that plays of Seneca, and plays in
imitation of Seneca, were being produced in Latin
at the Universities.[14] The *Troades* was performed in

[12] These facts are given succinctly in Cunliffe's *Influence of
Seneca.* The slight textual differences between the early editions
and that of 1581 are given by E. M. Spearing: *The Elizabethan
Translations of Seneca's Tragedies.*

[13] See E. M. Spearing: *op. cit.*

[14] For a convenient summary of the Senecan movement
throughout Europe, and particularly in England, see Kastner
and Charlton's edition of Alexander, above mentioned.

Latin at Trinity College, Cambridge, in 1551. Trinity resumed its enterprise in 1559—the year of Heywood's *Troas*—and between 1559 and 1561 the College produced in Latin four plays of Seneca. And during the 'sixties the two Universities first, and the Inns of Court subsequently, composed and performed a number of Latin plays on the Senecan model. This would have occurred, no doubt, even had Heywood never translated Seneca at all. But there can be little doubt that his translations indicate a nascent interest in a new vernacular drama to vie with classical drama, and that they in turn stimulated the beginning of this drama. At the same busy moment took place another event of capital importance, which combined with this Senecan work to produce English tragedy. In 1557 came the publication of Surrey's translation of Book II of the *Aeneid*, in the new "blank verse," the instrument without which the Elizabethan drama would have been impossible. The first-fruits, *Gorboduc*, are inconsiderable; but this play marks a new epoch; there is no clearer division in the whole of English literature.

We have, in fact, within a period of about forty years, three distinct phases in the development of English tragedy: the first, from 1559 to some time in the early 'eighties, is announced by Heywood's translations; the second is the period in which flourished Kyd and Peele, both of whom came to be influenced by the sudden and soon extinguished genius of Marlowe; the third is the period of Shakespeare up to his culminating tragedies. Then follows a period of Jacobian drama which belongs not so much to

Shakespeare, although Shakespeare's last plays fall
within the first years of it, as to Beaumont and
Fletcher: it is the period, not typically of tragedy,
but of tragicomic romance.

In the preceding section I insisted upon the difference between Seneca's influence upon popular drama
and his influence upon those fastidious spirits, the
Senecals, who tried to observe his dramatic laws. But
this difference of tendency is hardly apparent in the
first period, or until the appearance of Kyd and
Peele. During this period the fashions set at the
Universities were followed at the Inns of Court. The
plays produced by the legal wits were sometimes
acted at the Queen's Court, with which, indeed, the
Inns had a kind of formal connection. And in turn
the plays produced at the Royal Court affected the
more popular drama.[15] *Gorboduc* is followed by
Gismond of Salerne, and *Gismond* later by the popular and atrocious *Locrine* (in which Peele almost
certainly had a heavy hand); *The Misfortunes of
Arthur* was probably too tardy to play much part in
the transition. Another play of importance, which
shows the persistence of the influence from the Universities upon popular drama, is Legge's *Richardus
Tertius,* a Latin chronicle play acted at St. John's
College, Cambridge, in 1573, and apparently repeated in 1579 and 1582. This play is the parent of
The True Tragedy of Richard III, and consequently
of the entire brood of chronicle plays.

Another point which I have already considered,

[15] See J. M. Manly's introduction (p. v) to F. S. Miller's translation of *The Tragedies of Seneca* (1907).

but which must be mentioned here in a different context, is the relation of Seneca to *Italian* Seneca, and of both to the native tendencies of the time. Italian Seneca is not conspicuous until the period of Kyd and Peele; but even among the translations of Heywood we can find evidence that he was to be by no means unwelcome. Besides other peculiarities of these translations which we must examine, there is an interesting addition made by Heywood to the *Troas*. In the play of Seneca Achilles' Ghost makes no appearance; it is merely mentioned as having been seen. The play was the first to be translated, and there is some reason for believing that the translation was intended to be played. The "divers and sundrye" additions which Heywood invents render this supposition all the more plausible; for they are such as a translator would be much more likely to make if he had a performance in view, than if his translation were intended only for reading; in the latter event he might be expected to stick pretty closely to the text. Between the second and third acts of the *Troas* Heywood allows himself the liberty of interpolating a new scene of his own invention, which is a long soliloquy in thirteen stanzas by the Ghost of Achilles. And this independent "Sprite" rants in a tone which hardly Peele could outdo:

From burning lakes the furies wrath I threate,
And fire that nought but streames of bloud may slake
The rage of wind and seas their shippes shall beate,
And Ditis deepe on you shall vengeance take,
The sprites crye out, the earth and seas do quake,

The poole of Styx ungratefull Greekes it seath,
With slaughtred bloud revenge Achilles' death.

It is to be observed that Nevyle and Studley both
joined Inns of Court; that Nevyle came there to
know Gascoyne, the author of *Jocasta;* and that
Heywood knew, or at least knew of, Sackville and
Norton before they had written *Gorboduc.* The impulse toward the Tragedy of Blood is already
present in these translators, and they do not hesitate
to add or to alter; the distortion of Seneca begins
in his translation.

It is not only as an embryonic form of Elizabethan tragedy that these translations have documentary interest. They represent the transformation
of the older form of versification into the new—
consequently the transformation of language and
sensibility as well. Few things that can happen to a
nation are more important than the invention of a
new form of verse. And at no other time, and to no
other country than England at that time, has such an
achievement as that of Henry Howard, Earl of
Surrey, had greater consequences. To the French or
to the Italians it could not have mattered so much.
Their sensibility had already learned to express
itself in large part in prose: Boccaccio and Machiavelli in one country, and the chroniclers—Froissart,
Joinville, Commines—in the other, had already done
a great work in forming the local mind. But the
Elizabethan mind, far more than the contemporary
mind in any other country, grew and matured
through its verse rather than through its prose. The

development of prose between Elyot and Bacon is certainly remarkable; but a comparison of styles between, say, Latimer and Andrewes shows a slower rate of change than the same space of time in verse, or the same space of time in prose in the next century. On the other hand, a study of the styles, the syntax, and the cadences of blank verse from *Gorboduc* to Shakespeare, and even after Shakespeare in the work of Webster and Tourneur, brings to light a process which is wholly astonishing.

The *Tenne Tragedies* must have shown conclusively to the most sensitive contemporary ears that the fourteener had had its day; it was certain that the verse of Surrey's *Aeneid* was in every way the verse in which to render the dignity and pomposity of the Senecan rhythm. And the slower iambic pentameter brought with it an alteration in vocabulary. The fourteener had served very well in rough comedy; it runs jollily in *Roister Doister* and *Gammer Gurton*. It is no vehicle for solemn tragedy, and the miracle is that Heywood and Studley made as good a job with it as they did. The fourteener, and the kindred loose metres of the interlude, are not adapted to a highly Latinised vocabulary; they are adapted to a vocabulary containing a large proportion of short words and monosyllables of Germanic origin; a vocabulary which must have come to seem, as it seems to us, rather clownish, if fresh and vigorous. The language of early Tudor times is indeed in some ways a deterioration from the language of Chaucer. One reason for this is no doubt the change in pronunciation, the suppression of syllables; the melody of the older tongue had gone, and with this melody much of its dignity; new rhythms, and new infusions from abroad, were very much needed. At first, in fact, the innovations over-powered the language; the Elizabethan bombast was a verbal even more than an emotional debauch; it was not until the prose of Dryden and Hobbes that English settled down to something like sobriety.

In the *Iliad* of Chapman we see new wine bursting old bottles; the poem is a magnificent *tour de force* in which Chapman sometimes succeeds in fitting the new vocabulary to the old "stretched" metre. But it is, consequently, a poem of brilliant passages rather than sustained success. Heywood and Studley—particularly Studley—make no such attempt: their fourteener is early, not late Tudor; it is a different thing from Chapman's. Only in the pentameter rhymed choruses does their sensibility become more modern; the contrast between their dialogue and their chorus verse is interesting. Here is a random bit of Studley:

O wanny *jaws of Blacke Averne,* eake *Tartar
    dungeon grim,*
*O Lethes Lake of woful Soules the joy that therein
    swimme,*
And eake *ye* glummy *Gulphes destroy, destroy me
    wicked wight*
And still in pit of pangues *let me be plunged day
    and night.*
Now, now, come up ye Goblins grim from water
    creekes *alow . . .*

The majority of the rhyme words are monosyllables. The most sonorous and canorous Latin names are truncated (it remained for Marlowe to discover, and Milton to perfect, the musical possibilities of classical names almost to the point of *incantation*). Alliteration, in as primitive a form as that of *Piers Plowman,* is constant. For instance, Heywood has

> *shal Sisyphus his stone*
> *That slipper restles rollyng payse uppon my backe be*
>   *borne,*
> *Or shal my lymmes with swifter swinge of whirling*
>   *whele be torne?*
> *Or shal my paynes be Tytius panges th' encreasing*
>   *liver still,*
> *Whose growing guttes the gnawing gripes and fylthy*
>   *foules do fyll?*

To examine such lines under the microscope is not to do them justice; the vigorous vocabulary and swinging metre appear at their best when we read through a long descriptive or narrative passage: in the same play (the *Thyestes*) the messenger's account of the crime of Atreus (Act IV) is admirably rendered.

In their handling of the choruses the translators are less scrupulous. When they translate the dialogue they are literal to the best of their ability—occasional inaccuracies or mistranslations being admitted—but in the choruses they will sometimes lengthen or shorten, sometimes omit altogether, or substitute an invention of their own. On the whole, their alterations tend to make the play more dramatic; some-

times they may be suspected of adding a political
innuendo to the Senecan moralising on the vanity
of place and power. And it is especially in the
choruses that we find, now and then, flashes of that
felicity which is present in Tudor translation more
perhaps than in the translations of any period into
any language. For example, the whole of the chorus
at the end of Act IV of Heywood's *Hercules Furens*
is very fine, but the last six lines seem to me of
singular beauty; and as the original, too, is a lovely
passage, it is both fair and interesting to quote
original and translation. The persons addressed are
the dead children of Hercules, whom he has just
slain in his madness.

> *ite ad Stygios, umbrae, portus*
> *ite, innocues, quas in primo*
> *limine vitae scelus oppressit*
> *patriusque furor;*
> *ite, iratos visite reges.*

And Heywood:

> *Goe hurtles soules, whom mischiefe hath opprest*
> *Even in first porch of life but lately had,*
> *And fathers fury goe unhappy kind*
> *O litle children, by the way ful sad*
> > *Of journey knowen.*
> > *Goe see the angry kynges.*

Nothing can be said of such a translation except that
it is perfect. It is a last echo of the earlier tongue,
the language of Chaucer, with an overtone of that
Christian piety and pity which disappears with

Elizabethan verse. The greater part of the chorus work has not this purity: one feels a curious strain on the old vocabulary to say new things; the fluctuation, the shades of variation between the old world and the new deserve inquisitive study; the ambiguity probably contributes to give these translations a unique mood, which is only to be extracted and enjoyed after patient perusals. They are not translations to be read in a hurry; they do not yield their charm easily.

Such friendship finde wyth Gods yet no man myght,
That he the morowe might be sure to lyve.
The God our things all tost and turned quight
  Rolles with a whyrle wynde.

Christopher Marlowe

Swinburne observes of Marlowe that "the father of English tragedy and the creator of English blank verse was therefore also the teacher and the guide of Shakespeare." In this sentence there are two misleading assumptions and two misleading conclusions. Kyd has as good a title to the first honour as Marlowe; Surrey has a better title to the second; and Shakespeare was not taught or guided by one of his predecessors or contemporaries alone. The less questionable judgment is, that Marlowe exercised a strong influence over later drama, though not himself as great a dramatist as Kyd; that he introduced several new tones into blank verse, and commenced the dissociative process which drew it farther and farther away from the rhythms of rhymed verse; and that when Shakespeare borrowed from him, which was pretty often at the beginning, Shakespeare either made something inferior or something different.

The comparative study of English versification at various periods is a large tract of unwritten history. To make a study of blank verse alone would be to elicit

some curious conclusions. It would show, I believe,
that blank verse within Shakespeare's lifetime was
more highly developed, that it became the vehicle
of more varied and more intense feeling than it has
ever conveyed since; and that after the erection of
the Chinese Wall of Milton, blank verse has suffered
not only arrest but retrogression. That the blank
verse of Tennyson, for example, a consummate
master of this form in certain applications, is cruder
(*not* "rougher" or less perfect in technique) than that
of half a dozen contemporaries of Shakespeare;
cruder, because less capable of expressing complicated, subtle, and surprising emotions.

Every writer who has written any blank verse
worth saving has produced particular tones which
his verse and no other's is capable of rendering; and
we should keep this in mind when we talk about
"influences" and "indebtedness." Shakespeare is "universal" because he has more of these tones than any
one else; but they are all out of the one man; one
man cannot be more than one man; there might
have been six Shakespeares at once without conflict-
ing frontiers; and to say that Shakespeare expressed
nearly all human emotions, implying that he left
very little for any one else, is a radical misunderstanding of art and the artist—a misunderstanding
which, even when explicitly rejected, may lead to
our neglecting the effort of attention necessary to
discover the specific properties of the verse of Shakespeare's contemporaries. The development of blank
verse may be likened to the analysis of that astonishing industrial product coal-tar. Marlowe's verse is

one of the earlier derivatives, but it possesses properties which are not repeated in any of the analytic
or synthetic blank verses discovered somewhat later.

The "vices of style" of Marlowe's and Shakespeare's age is a convenient name for a number of
vices, no one of which, perhaps, was shared by all of
the writers. It is pertinent, at least, to remark that
Marlowe's "rhetoric" is not, or not characteristically,
Shakespeare's rhetoric; that Marlowe's rhetoric
consists in a pretty simple huffe-snuffe bombast,
while Shakespeare's is more exactly a vice of style,
a tortured perverse ingenuity of images which dissi-
pates instead of concentrating the imagination, and
which may be due in part to influences by which
Marlowe was untouched. Next, we find that Marlowe's vice is one which he was gradually attenuating,
and even, what is more miraculous, turning into a
virtue. And we find that this poet of torrential
imagination recognized many of his best bits (and
those of one or two others), saved them, and repro-
duced them more than once, almost invariably
improving them in the process.

It is worth while noticing a few of these versions,
because they indicate, somewhat contrary to usual
opinion, that Marlowe was a deliberate and conscious
workman. Mr. J. M. Robertson has spotted an interesting theft of Marlowe's from Spenser. Here
is Spenser (*Faerie Queene,* I, vii, 32):

Like to an almond tree y-mounted high
   On top of green Selinis all alone,
With blossoms brave bedeckèd daintily;

> *Whose tender locks do tremble every one*
> *At every little breath that under heaven is blown.*

And here Marlowe (*Tamburlaine,* Part II, Act IV, sc. iv):

> *Like to an almond tree y-mounted high*
> *Upon the lofty and celestial mount*
> *Of evergreen Selinus, quaintly deck'd*
> *With blooms more white than Erycina's brows,*
> *Whose tender blossoms tremble every one*
> *At every little breath that thorough heaven is blown.*

This is interesting, not only as showing that Marlowe's talent, like that of most poets, was partly synthetic, but also because it seems to give a clue to some particularly "lyric" effects found in *Tamburlaine,* not in Marlowe's other plays, and not, I believe, anywhere else. For example, the praise of Zenocrate in Part II, Act II, sc. iv:

> *Now walk the angels on the walls of heaven,*
> *As sentinels to warn th' immortal souls*
> *To entertain divine Zenocrate.*

This is not Spenser's movement, but the influence of Spenser must be present. There had been no great blank verse before Marlowe; but there was the powerful presence of this great master of melody immediately precedent; and the combination produced results which could not be repeated. I do not think that it can be claimed that Peel had any influence here.

The passage quoted from Spenser has a further interest. It will be noted that the fourth line:

With blooms more white than Erycina's brows,

is Marlowe's contribution. Compare this with these other lines of Marlowe:

> *So looks my love, shadowing in her brows*
> *(Tamburlaine)*
> *Like to the shadows of Pyramides*
> *(Tamburlaine)*

and the final and best version:

> *Shadowing more beauty in their airy brows*
> *Than have the white breasts of the queen of love*
> *(Doctor Faustus)*

and compare the whole set with Spenser again (*F. Q.*):

> *Upon her eyelids many graces sate*
> *Under the shadow of her even brows,*

a passage which Mr. Robertson says Spenser himself used in three other places.

This economy is frequent in Marlowe. Within *Tamburlaine* it occurs in the form of monotony, especially in the facile use of resonant names (*e.g.* the recurrence of "Caspia" or "Caspian" with the same tone effect), a practice in which Marlowe was followed by Milton, but which Marlowe himself outgrew. Again,

> *Zenocrate, lovelier than the love of Jove,*
> *Brighter than is the silver Rhodope,*

is paralleled later by

> Zenocrate, the loveliest maid alive,
> Fairer than rocks of pearl and precious stone.

One line Marlowe remodels with triumphant success:

> And set black streamers in the firmament
>
> > (Tamburlaine)

becomes

> See, see, where Christ's blood streams in the firmament!
>
> > (Doctor Faustus)

The verse accomplishments of *Tamburlaine* are notably two: Marlowe gets into blank verse the melody of Spenser, and he gets a new driving power by reinforcing the sentence period against the line period. The rapid long sentence, running line into line, as in the famous soliloquies "Nature compounded of four elements" and "What is beauty, saith my sufferings, then?" marks the certain escape of blank verse from the rhymed couplet, and from the elegiac or rather pastoral note of Surrey, to which Tennyson returned. If you contrast these two soliloquies with the verse of Marlowe's greatest contemporary, Kyd—by no means a despicable versifier—you see the importance of the innovation:

> The one took sanctuary, and, being sent for out,
> Was murdered in Southwark as he passed
> To Greenwich, where the Lord Protector lay.
> Black Will was burned in Flushing on a stage;
> Green was hanged at Osbridge in Kent . . .

which is not really inferior to:

> *So these four abode*
> *Within one house together; and as years*
> *Went forward, Mary took another mate;*
> *But Dora lived unmarried till her death.*
>
> (TENNYSON, *Dora*)

In *Faustus* Marlowe went farther: he broke up the line, to a gain in intensity, in the last soliloquy; and he developed a new and important conversational tone in the dialogues of Faustus with the devil. *Edward II* has never lacked consideration: it is more desirable, in brief space, to remark upon two plays, one of which has been misunderstood and the other underrated. These are *The Jew of Malta* and *Dido Queen of Carthage*. Of the first of these, it has always been said that the end, even the last two acts, are unworthy of the first three. If one takes *The Jew of Malta* not as a tragedy, or as a "tragedy of blood," but as a farce, the concluding act becomes intelligible; and if we attend with a careful ear to the versification, we find that Marlowe develops a tone to suit this farce, and even perhaps that this tone is his most powerful and mature tone. I say farce, but with the enfeebled humour of our times the word is a misnomer; it is the farce of the old English humour, the terribly serious, even savage comic humour, the humour which spent its last breath in the decadent genius of Dickens. It has nothing in common with J. M. Barrie, Captain Bairnsfather, or *Punch*. It is the humour of that very serious (but very different) play, *Volpone*.

> *First, be thou void of these affections,*
> *Compassion, love, vain hope, and heartless fear;*
> *Be moved at nothing, see thou pity none . . .*
> *As for myself, I walk abroad o' nights,*
> *And kill sick people groaning under walls,*
> *Sometimes I go about and poison wells . . .*

and the last words of Barabas complete this prodigious caricature:

> *But now begins th' extremity of heat*
> *To pinch me with intolerable pangs,*
> *Die, life! fly, soul! tongue, curse thy fill, and die!*

It is something which Shakespeare could not do, and which he did not want to do.

Dido appears to be a hurried play, perhaps done to order with the *Aeneid* in front of him. But even here there is progress. The account of the sack of Troy is in this newer style of Marlowe's, this style which secures its emphasis by always hesitating on the edge of caricature at the right moment:

The Grecian soldiers, tir'd with ten years' war,
Began to cry, "Let us unto our ships,
Troy is invincible, why stay we here?" . . .

By this, the camp was come unto the walls,
And through the breach did march into the streets,
Where, meeting with the rest, "Kill, kill!" they
 cried. . . .

And after him, his band of Myrmidons,
With balls of wild-fire in their murdering paws . . .

At last, the soldiers pull'd her by the heels,
And swung her howling in the empty air. . . .

We saw Cassandra sprawling in the streets . . .

This is not Virgil, or Shakespeare; it is pure Mar-
'lowe. By comparing the whole speech with Clarence's
dream, in *Richard III,* one acquires a little insight
into the difference between Marlowe and Shakespeare:

> *What scourge for perjury*
> *Can this dark monarchy afford false Clarence?*

There, on the other hand, is what Marlowe's style
could not do; the phrase has a concision which is
almost classical, certainly Dantesque. Again, as often
with the Elizabethan dramatists, there are lines in
Marlowe, besides the many lines that Shakespeare
adapted, that might have been written by either:

> *If thou wilt stay,*
> *Leap in mine arms; mine arms are open wide;*
> *If not, turn from me, and I'll turn from thee;*
> *For though thou hast the heart to say farewell,*
> *I have not power to stay thee.*

But the direction in which Marlowe's verse might
have moved, had he not "dyed swearing," is quite
un-Shakespearean, is toward this intense and serious
and indubitably great poetry, which, like some great
painting and sculpture, attains its effects by something not unlike caricature.

Ben Jonson

The reputation of Jonson has been of the most deadly kind that can be compelled upon the memory of a great poet. To be universally accepted; to be damned by the praise that quenches all desire to read the book; to be afflicted by the imputation of the virtues which excite the least pleasure; and to be read only by historians and antiquaries—this is the most perfect conspiracy of approval. For some generations the reputation of Jonson has been carried rather as a liability than as an asset in the balance-sheet of English literature. No critic has succeeded in making him appear pleasurable or even interesting. Swinburne's book on Jonson satisfies no curiosity and stimulates no thought. For the critical study in the "Men of Letters Series" by Mr. Gregory Smith there is a place; it satisfies curiosity, it supplies many just observations, it provides valuable matter on the neglected masques; it only fails to remodel the image of Jonson which is settled in our minds. Probably the fault lies with several generations of our poets. It is not that the value of poetry is only its value to living poets for their own work; but appreciation is

akin to creation, and true enjoyment of poetry is
related to the stirring of suggestion, the stimulus
that a poet feels in his enjoyment of other poetry.
Jonson has provided no creative stimulus for a very
long time; consequently we must look back as far as
Dryden—precisely, a poetic practitioner who learned
from Jonson—before we find a living criticism of
Jonson's work.

Yet there are possibilities for Jonson even now.
We have no difficulty in seeing what brought him
to this pass; how, in contrast, not with Shakespeare,
but with Marlowe, Webster, Donne, Beaumont, and
Fletcher, he has been paid out with reputation
instead of enjoyment. He is no less a poet than these
men, but his poetry is of the surface. Poetry of the
surface cannot be understood without study; for to
deal with the surface of life, as Jonson dealt with it,
is to deal so deliberately that we too must be
deliberate, in order to understand. Shakespeare, and
smaller men also, are in the end more difficult, but
they offer something at the start to encourage the
student or to satisfy those who want nothing more;
they are suggestive, evocative, a phrase, a voice; they
offer poetry in detail as well as in design. So does
Dante offer something, a phrase everywhere (*tu se'
ombra ed ombra vedi*) even to readers who have no
Italian; and Dante and Shakespeare have poetry of
design as well as of detail. But the polished veneer
of Jonson reflects only the lazy reader's fatuity;
unconscious does not respond to unconscious; no
swarms of inarticulate feelings are aroused. The immediate appeal of Jonson is to the mind; his

emotional tone is not in the single verse, but in the design of the whole. But not many people are capable of discovering for themselves the beauty which is only found after labour; and Jonson's industrious readers have been those whose interest was historical and curious, and those who have thought that in discovering the historical and curious interest they had discovered the artistic value as well. When we say that Jonson requires study, we do not mean study of his classical scholarship or of seventeenth-century manners. We mean intelligent saturation in his work as a whole; we mean that in order to enjoy him at all, we must get to the centre of his work and his temperament, and that we must see him unbiased by time, as a contemporary. And to see him as a contemporary does not so much require the power of putting ourselves into seventeenth-century London as it requires the power of setting Jonson in our London.

It is generally conceded that Jonson failed as a tragic dramatist; and it is usually agreed that he failed because his genius was for satiric comedy and because of the weight of pedantic learning with which he burdened his two tragic failures. The second point marks an obvious error of detail; the first is too crude a statement to be accepted; to say that he failed because his genius was unsuited to tragedy is to tell us nothing at all. Jonson did not write a good tragedy, but we can see no reason why he should not have written one. If two plays so different as *The Tempest* and *The Silent Woman* are both comedies, surely the category of tragedy

could be made wide enough to include something
possible for Jonson to have done. But the classification of tragedy and comedy, while it may be sufficient
to mark the distinction in a dramatic literature of
more rigid form and treatment—it may distinguish
Aristophanes from Euripides—is not adequate to a
drama of such variations as the Elizabethans'. Tragedy is a crude classification for plays so different in
their tone as *Macbeth, The Jew of Malta,* and *The
Witch of Edmonton;* and it does not help us much
to say that *The Merchant of Venice* and *The
Alchemist* are comedies. Jonson had his own scale,
his own instrument. The merit which *Catiline*
possesses is the same merit that is exhibited more
triumphantly in *Volpone; Catiline* fails, not because
it is too laboured and conscious, but because it is
not conscious enough; because Jonson in this play
was not alert to his own idiom, not clear in his mind
as to what his temperament wanted him to do. In
Catiline Jonson conforms, or attempts to conform,
to conventions; not to the conventions of antiquity,
which he had exquisitely under control, but to the
conventions of tragico-historical drama of his time.
It is not the Latin erudition that sinks *Catiline,* but
the application of that erudition to a form which
was not the proper vehicle for the mind which had
amassed the erudition.

If you look at *Catiline*—that dreary Pyrrhic victory
of tragedy—you find two passages to be successful:
Act II, sc. i, the dialogue of the political ladies, and
the Prologue of Sylla's ghost. These two passages are

genial. The soliloquy of the ghost is a characteristic
Jonson success in content and in versification—

Dost thou not feel me, Rome? not yet! is night
So heavy on thee, and my weight so light?
Can Sylla's ghost arise within thy walls,
Less threatening than an earthquake, the quick falls
Of thee and thine? Shake not the frighted heads
Of thy steep towers, or shrink to their first beds?
Or as their ruin the large Tyber fills,
Make that swell up, and drown thy seven proud
   hills? . . .

This is the learned, but also the creative, Jonson.
Without concerning himself with the character of
Sulla, and in lines of invective, Jonson makes Sylla's
ghost, while the words are spoken, a living and
terrible force. The words fall with as determined
beat as if they were the will of the morose Dictator
himself. You may say: merely invective; but mere
invective, even if as superior to the clumsy fisticuffs
of Marston and Hall as Jonson's verse is superior
to theirs, would not create a living figure as Jonson
has done in this long tirade And you may say: rhetoric; but if we are to call it "rhetoric" we must subject that term to a closer dissection than any to which
it is accustomed. What Jonson has done here is not
merely a fine speech. It is the careful, precise filling
in of a strong and simple outline, and at no point
does it overflow the outline; it is far more careful
and precise in its obedience to this outline than
are many of the speeches in *Tamburlaine*. The out-

line is not Sulla, for Sulla has nothing to do with it, but "Sylla's ghost." The words may not be suitable to an historical Sulla, or to anybody in history, but they are a perfect expression for "Sylla's ghost." You cannot say they are rhetorical "because people do not talk like that," you cannot call them "verbiage"; they do not exhibit prolixity or redundancy or the other vices in the rhetoric books; there is a definite artistic emotion which demands expression at that length. The words themselves are mostly simple words, the syntax is natural, the language austere rather than adorned. Turning then to the induction of *The Poetaster*, we find another success of the same kind—

Light, I salute thee, but with wounded nerves . . .

Men may not talk in that way, but the Spirit of Envy does, and in the words of Jonson envy is a real and living person. It is not human life that informs envy and Sylla's ghost, but it is energy of which human life is only another variety.

Returning to *Catiline*, we find that the best scene in the body of the play is one which cannot be squeezed into a tragic frame, and which appears to belong to satiric comedy. The scene between Fulvia and Galla and Sempronia is a living scene in a wilderness of oratory. And as it recalls other scenes— there is a suggestion of the college of ladies in *The Silent Woman*—it looks like a comedy scene. And it appears to be satire.

They shall all give and pay well, that come here,
If they will have it; and that, jewels, pearl,

Plate, or round sums to buy these. I'm not taken
With a cob-swan or a high-mounting bull,
As foolish Leda and Europa were;
But the bright gold, with Danaë. For such price
I would endure a rough, harsh Jupiter,
Or ten such thundering gamesters, and refrain
To laugh at 'em, till they are gone, with my much
    suffering.

This scene is no more comedy than it is tragedy, and the "satire" is merely a medium for the essential emotion. Jonson's drama is only incidentally satire, because it is only incidentally a criticism upon the actual world. It is not satire in the way in which the work of Swift or the work of Molière may be called satire: that is, it does not find its source in any precise emotional attitude or precise intellectual criticism of the actual world. It is satire perhaps as the work of Rabelais is satire; certainly not more so. The important thing is that if fiction can be divided into creative fiction and critical fiction, Jonson's is creative. That he was a great critic, our first great critic, does not affect this assertion. Every creator is also a critic; Jonson was a conscious critic, but he was also conscious in his creations. Certainly, one sense in which the term "critical" may be applied to fiction is a sense in which the term might be used of a method antithetical to Jonson's. It is the method of *Education Sentimentale*. The characters of Jonson, of Shakespeare, perhaps of all the greatest drama, are drawn in positive and simple outlines. They may be filled in, and by Shakespeare they are filled in, by much detail or many shifting aspects; but a clear and sharp and simple form remains through these—though it would be hard to say in what the clarity and sharpness and simplicity of Hamlet consists. But Frédéric Moreau is not made in that way. He is constructed partly by negative definition, built up by a great number of observations. We cannot isolate him from the environment in which we find him; it may be an environment which is or can be universalized; nevertheless it and the figure in it consist of very many observed particular facts, the actual world. Without this world the figure dissolves. The ruling faculty is a critical perception, a commentary upon experienced feeling and sensation. If this is true of Flaubert, it is true in a higher degree of Molière than of Jonson. The broad farcical lines of Molière may seem to be the same drawing as Jonson's. But Molière—say in Alceste or Monsieur Jourdain—is criticizing the actual; the reference to the actual world is more direct. And having a more tenuous reference, the work of Jonson is much less directly satirical.

This leads us to the question of Humours. Largely on the evidence of the two Humour plays, it is sometimes assumed that Jonson is occupied with types; typical exaggerations, or exaggerations of type. The Humour definition, the expressed intention of Jonson, may be satisfactory for these two plays. *Every Man in his Humour* is the first mature work of Jonson, and the student of Jonson must study it; but it is not the play in which Jonson found his genius: it is the last of his plays to read first. If one reads *Volpone*, and after that re-reads *The Jew of Malta;* then returns to Jonson and reads *Bartholomew Fair, The Alchemist, Epicoene* and *The Devil is an Ass,* and finally *Catiline,* it is possible to arrive at a fair opinion of the poet and the dramatist.

The Humour, even at the beginning, is not a type, as in Marston's satire, but a simplified and somewhat distorted individual with a typical mania. In the later work, the Humour definition quite fails to account for the total effect produced. The characters of Shakespeare are such as might exist in different circumstances than those in which Shakespeare sets them. The latter appear to be those which extract from the characters the most intense and interesting realization; but that realization has not exhausted their possibilities. Volpone's life, on the other hand, is bounded by the scene in which it is played; in fact, the life is the life of the scene and is derivatively the life of Volpone; the life of the character is inseparable from the life of the drama. This is not dependence upon a background, or upon a substratum of fact. The emotional effect is single and simple. Whereas in Shakespeare the effect is due to the way in which the characters *act upon* one another, in Jonson it is given by the way in which the characters *fit in* with each other. The artistic result of *Volpone* is not due to any effect that Volpone, Mosca, Corvino, Corbaccio, Voltore have upon each other, but simply to their combination into a whole. And these figures are not personifications of passions; separately, they have not even that reality, they are constitu-

ents. It is a similar indication of Jonson's method
that you can hardly pick out a line of Jonson's and
say confidently that it is great poetry; but there are
many extended passages to which you cannot deny
that honour.

> *I will have all my beds blown up, not stuft;*
> *Down is too hard; and then, mine oval room*
> *Fill'd with such pictures as Tiberius took*
> *From Elephantis, and dull Aretine*
> *But coldly imitated. Then, my glasses*
> *Cut in more subtle angles, to disperse*
> *And multiply the figures, as I walk. . . .*

Jonson is the legitimate heir of Marlowe. The
man who wrote, in *Volpone:*

> *for thy love,*
> *In varying figures, I would have contended*
> *With the blue Proteus, or the hornèd flood. . . .*

and

> *See, a carbuncle*
> *May put out both the eyes of our Saint Mark;*
> *A diamond would have bought Lollia Paulina,*
> *When she came in like star-light, hid with jewels. . . .*

is related to Marlowe as a poet; and if Marlowe is a
poet, Jonson is also. And, if Jonson's comedy is a
comedy of humours, then Marlowe's tragedy, a large
part of it, is a tragedy of humours. But Jonson has
too exclusively been considered as the typical repre-
sentative of a point of view toward comedy. He has
suffered from his great reputation as a critic and

theorist, from the effects of his intelligence. We
have been taught to think of him as the man, the
dictator (confusedly in our minds with his later
namesake), as the literary politician impressing his
views upon a generation; we are offended by the constant reminder of his scholarship. We forget the
comedy in the humours, and the serious artist in the
scholar. Jonson has suffered in public opinion, as
any one must suffer who is forced to talk about his
art.

If you examine the first hundred lines or more of
Volpone the verse appears to be in the manner of
Marlowe, more deliberate, more mature, but without
Marlowe's inspiration. It looks like mere "rhetoric,"
certainly not "deeds and language such as men do
use." It appears to us, in fact, forced and flagitious
bombast. That it is not "rhetoric," or at least not
vicious rhetoric, we do not know until we are able
to review the whole play. For the consistent maintenance of this manner conveys in the end an effect
not of verbosity, but of bold, even shocking and terri-
fying directness. We have difficulty in saying exactly
what produces this simple and single effect. It is not
in any ordinary way due to management of intrigue.
Jonson employs immense dramatic constructive skill:
it is not so much skill in plot as skill in doing without a plot. He never manipulates as complicated a
plot as that of *The Merchant of Venice*; he has in
his best plays nothing like the intrigue of Restoration
comedy. In *Bartholomew Fair* it is hardly a plot at
all; the marvel of the play is the bewildering rapid
chaotic action of the fair; it is the fair itself, not

anything that happens in the fair. In *Volpone,* or *The Alchemist,* or *The Silent Woman,* the plot is enough to keep the players in motion; it is rather an "action" than a plot. The plot does not hold the play together; what holds the play together is a unity of inspiration that radiates into plot and personages alike.

We have attempted to make more precise the sense in which it was said that Jonson's work is "of the surface"; carefully avoiding the word "superficial." For there is work contemporary with Jonson's which is superficial in a pejorative sense in which the word cannot be applied to Jonson—the work of Beaumont and Fletcher. If we look at the work of Jonson's great contemporaries, Shakespeare, and also Donne and Webster and Tourneur (and sometimes Middleton), they have a depth, a third dimension, as Mr. Gregory Smith rightly calls it, which Jonson's work has not. Their words have often a network of tentacular roots reaching down to the deepest terrors and desires. Jonson's most certainly have not; but in Beaumont and Fletcher we may think that at times we find it. Looking closer, we discover that the blossoms of Beaumont and Fletcher's imagination draw no sustenance from the soil, but are cut and slightly withered flowers stuck into sand.

Wilt thou, hereafter, when they talk of me,
As thou shalt hear nothing but infamy,
Remember some of these things? . . .
I pray thee, do; for thou shalt never see me so again.

Hair woven in many a curious warp,
Able in endless error to enfold
The wandering soul; . . .

Detached from its context, this looks like the verse of the greater poets; just as lines of Jonson, detached from their context, look like inflated or empty fustian. But the evocative quality of the verse of Beaumont and Fletcher depends upon a clever appeal to emotions and associations which they have not themselves grasped; it is hollow. It is superficial with a vacuum behind it; the superficies of Jonson is solid. It is what it is; it does not pretend to be another thing. But it is so very conscious and deliberate that we must look with eyes alert to the whole before we apprehend the significance of any part. We cannot call a man's work superficial when it is the creation of a world; a man cannot be accused of dealing superficially with the world which he himself has created; the superficies *is* the world. Jonson's characters conform to the logic of the emotions of their world. They are not fancy, because they have a logic of their own; and this logic illuminates the actual world, because it gives us a new point of view from which to inspect it.

A writer of power and intelligence, Jonson endeavoured to promulgate, as a formula and programme of reform, what he chose to do himself; and he not unnaturally laid down in abstract theory what is in reality a personal point of view. And it is in the end of no value to discuss Jonson's theory and

practice unless we recognize and seize this point of
view, which escapes the formulae, and which is what
makes his plays worth reading. Jonson behaved as
the great creative mind that he was: he created his
own world, a world from which his followers, as well
as the dramatists who were trying to do something
wholly different, are excluded. Remembering this, we
turn to Mr. Gregory Smith's objection—that Jonson's
characters lack the third dimension, have no life out
of the theatrical existence in which they appear—
and demand an inquest. The objection implies
that the characters are purely the work of intellect,
or the result of superficial observation of a world
which is faded or mildewed. It implies that the characters are lifeless. But if we dig beneath the theory,
beneath the observation, beneath the deliberate
drawing and the theatrical and dramatic elaboration,
there is discovered a kind of power, animating
Volpone, Busy, Fitzdottrel, the literary ladies of
Epicoene, even Bobadil, which comes from below the
intellect, and for which no theory of humours will
account. And it is the same kind of power which
vivifies Trimalchio, and Panurge, and some but not
all of the "comic" characters of Dickens. The fictive
life of this kind is not to be circumscribed by a
reference to "comedy" or to "farce"; it is not exactly the kind of life which informs the characters
of Molière or that which informs those of Marivaux
—two writers who were, besides, doing something
quite different the one from the other. But it is something which distinguishes Barabas from Shylock,
Epicure Mammon from Falstaff, Faustus from—if

you will—Macbeth; Marlowe and Jonson from Shakespeare and the Shakespeareans, Webster, and Tourneur. It is not merely Humours: for neither Volpone nor Mosca is a humour. No theory of humours could account for Jonson's best plays or the best characters in them. We want to know at what point the comedy of humours passes into a work of art, and why Jonson is not Brome.

The creation of a work of art, we will say the creation of a character in a drama, consists in the process of transfusion of the personality, or, in a deeper sense, the life, of the author into the character. This is a very different matter from the orthodox creation in one's own image. The ways in which the passions and desires of the creator may be satisfied in the work of art are complex and devious. In a painter they may take the form of a predilection for certain colours, tones, or lightings; in a writer the original impulse may be even more strangely transmuted. Now, we may say with Mr. Gregory Smith that Falstaff or a score of Shakespeare's characters have a "third dimension" that Jonson's have not. This will mean, not that Shakespeare's spring from the feelings or imagination and Jonson's from the intellect or invention; they have equally an emotional source; but that Shakespeare's represent a more complex tissue of feelings and desires, as well as a more supple, a more susceptible temperament. Falstaff is not only the roast Manningtree ox with the pudding in his belly; he also "grows old," and, finally, his nose is as sharp as a pen. He was perhaps the *satisfaction* of more, and of more complicated

feelings; and perhaps he was, as the great tragic
characters must have been, the offspring of deeper,
less apprehensible feelings: deeper, but not necessarily stronger or more intense, than those of Jonson.
It is obvious that the spring of the difference is not
the difference between feeling and thought, or superior insight, superior perception, on the part of
Shakespeare, but his suceptibility to a greater range
of emotion, and emotion deeper and more obscure.
But his characters are no more "alive" than are the
characters of Jonson.

The world they live in is a larger one. But small
worlds—the worlds which artists create—do not differ
only in magnitude; if they are complete worlds,
drawn to scale in every part, they differ in kind also.
And Jonson's world has this scale. His type of personality found its relief in something falling under
the category of burlesque or farce—though when
you are dealing with a *unique* world, like his, these
terms fail to appease the desire for definition. It is
not, at all events, the farce of Molière: the latter is
more analytic, more an intellectual redistribution.
It is not defined by the word "satire." Jonson poses
as a satirist. But satire like Jonson's is great in the
end not by hitting off its object, but by creating it;
the satire is merely the means which leads to the
aesthetic result, the impulse which projects a new
world into a new orbit. In *Every Man in his Humour*
there is a neat, a very neat, comedy of humours. In
discovering and proclaiming in this play the new
genre Jonson was simply recognizing, unconsciously,
the route which opened out in the proper direction

for his instincts. His characters are and remain, like
Marlowe's, simplified characters; but the simplification does not consist in the dominance of a particular humour or monomania. That is a very
superficial account of it. The simplification consists
largely in reduction of detail, in the seizing of aspects
relevant to the relief of an emotional impulse which
remains the same for that character, in making the
character conform to a particular setting. This strip-
ping is essential to the art, to which is also essential
a flat distortion in the drawing; it is an art of caricature, of great caricature, like Marlowe's. It is a great
caricature, which is beautiful; and a great humour,
which is serious. The "world" of Jonson is sufficiently
large; it is a world of poetic imagination; it is
sombre. He did not get the third dimension, but he
was not trying to get it.

If we approach Jonson with less frozen awe of his
learning, with a clearer understanding of his "rhetoric" and its applications, if we grasp the fact that the
knowledge required of the reader is not archaeology
but knowledge of Jonson, we can derive not only
instruction in two-dimensional life—but enjoyment.
We can even apply him, be aware of him as a part
of our literary inheritance craving further expression.
Of all the dramatists of his time, Jonson is probably
the one whom the present age would find the most
sympathetic, if it knew him. There is a brutality, a
lack of sentiment, a polished surface, a handling of
large bold designs in brilliant colours, which ought
to attract about three thousand people in London
and elsewhere. At least, if we had a contemporary

Shakespeare and a contemporary Jonson, it might be
the Jonson who would arouse the enthusiasm of the
intelligentsia. Though he is saturated in literature,
he never sacrifices the theatrical qualities—theatrical
in the most favourable sense—to literature or to the
study of character. His work is a titanic show. But
Jonson's masques, an important part of his work, are
neglected; our flaccid culture lets shows and literature fade, but prefers faded literature to faded
shows. There are hundreds of people who have read
Comus to ten who have read the *Masque of Black-
ness. Comus* contains fine poetry, and poetry exempli-
fying some merits to which Jonson's masque poetry
cannot pretend. Nevertheless, *Comus* is the death of
the masque; it is the transition of a form of art—
even of a form which existed for but a short generation—into "literature," literature cast in a form
which has lost its application. Even though *Comus*
was a masque at Ludlow Castle, Jonson had, what
Milton came perhaps too late to have, a sense for the
living art; his art was applied. The masques can still
be read, and with pleasure, by any one who will take
the trouble—a trouble which in this part of Jonson
is, indeed, a study of antiquities—to imagine them
in action, displayed with the music, costumes, dances,
and the scenery of Inigo Jones. They are additional
evidence that Jonson had a fine sense of form, of the
purpose for which a particular form is intended; evidence that he was a literary artist even more than he
was a man of letters.

Thomas Middleton

Thomas Middleton, the dramatic writer, was not very highly thought of in his own time; the date of his death is not known; we know only that he was buried on July 4, 1627. He was one of the most voluminous, and one of the best, dramatic writers of his time. But it is easy to understand why he is not better known or more popular. It is difficult to imagine his "personality." Several new personalities have recently been fitted to the name of Shakespeare; Jonson is a real figure—our imagination plays about him discoursing at the Mermaid, or laying down the law to Drummond of Hawthornden; Chapman has become a breezy British character as firm as Nelson or Wellington; Webster and Donne are real people for the more intellectual; even Tourneur (Churton Collins having said the last word about him) is a "personality." But Middleton, who collaborated shamelessly, who is hardly separated from Rowley, Middleton who wrote plays so diverse as *Women Beware Women* and *A Game at Chesse* and *The Roaring Girle,* Middleton remains merely a collective name for a number of plays—some of which, like *The Spanish Gipsie,* are patently by other people.[1]

If we write about Middleton's plays we must write about Middleton's plays, and not about Middleton's personality. Many of these plays are still in doubt. Of all the Elizabethan dramatists Middleton seems the most impersonal, the most indifferent to personal fame or perpetuity, the readiest, except Rowley, to accept collaboration. Also he is the most various. His greatest tragedies and his greatest comedies are as if written by two different men. Yet there seems no doubt that Middleton was both a great comic writer and a great tragic writer. There are a sufficient number of plays, both tragedies and comedies, in which his hand is so far unquestioned, to establish his greatness. His greatness is not that of a peculiar personality, but of a great artist or artisan of the Elizabethan epoch. We have among others *The Changeling, Women Beware Women,* and *A Game at Chesse;* and we have *The Roaring Girle* and *A Trick to Catch the Old One.* And that is enough. Between the tragedies and the comedies of Shakespeare, and certainly between the tragedies and the comedies of Jonson, we can establish a relation; we can see, for Shakespeare or Jonson, that each had in the end a personal point of view which can be called neither comic nor tragic. But with Middleton we can establish no such relation. He remains merely a name, a voice, the author of certain plays, which are all of them great plays.

[1] Mr. Dugdale Sykes has written authoritatively on this subject.

He has no point of view, is neither sentimental nor cynical; he is neither resigned, nor disillusioned, nor romantic, he has no message. He is merely the name which associates six or seven great plays.

For there is no doubt about *The Changeling*. Like all of the plays attributed to Middleton, it is long-winded and tiresome; the characters talk too much, and then suddenly stop talking and act; they are real and impelled irresistibly by the fundamental motions of humanity to good or evil. This mixture of tedious discourse and sudden reality is everywhere in the work of Middleton, in his comedy also. In *The Roaring Girle* we read with toil through a mass of cheap conventional intrigue, and suddenly realize that we are, and have been for some time without knowing it, observing a real and unique human being. In reading *The Changeling* we may think, till almost the end of the play, that we have been concerned merely with a fantastic Elizabethan morality, and then discover that we are looking on at a dispassionate exposure of fundamental passions of any time and any place. The usual opinion remains the just judgment: *The Changeling* is Middleton's greatest play. The morality of the convention seems to us absurd. To many intelligent readers this play has only an historical interest, and only serves to illustrate the moral taboos of the Elizabethans. The heroine is a young woman who, in order to dispose of a fiancé to whom she is indifferent, so that she may marry the man she loves, accepts the offer of an adventurer to murder the affianced, at the price (as she finds in due course) of becoming the murderer's mistress. Such a plot is, to a modern mind, absurd; and the consequent tragedy seems a fuss about nothing. But *The Changeling* is not merely contingent for its effect upon our acceptance of Elizabethan good form or convention; it is, in fact, no more dependent upon the convention of its epoch than a play like *A Doll's House.* Underneath the convention there is the stratum of truth permanent in human nature. The tragedy of *The Changeling* is an eternal tragedy, as permanent as *Oedipus* or *Antony and Cleopatra;* it is the tragedy of the not naturally bad but irresponsible and undeveloped nature, caught in the consequences of its own action. In every age and in every civilization there are instances of the same thing: the unmoral nature, suddenly trapped in the inexorable toils of morality—of morality not made by man but by Nature—and forced to take the consequences of an act which it had planned lightheartedly. Beatrice is not a moral creature; she becomes moral only by becoming damned. Our conventions are not the same as those which Middleton assumed for his play. But the possibility of that frightful discovery of morality remains permanent.

The words in which Middleton expresses his tragedy are as great as the tragedy. The process through which Beatrice, having decided that De Flores is the instrument for her purpose, passes from aversion to habituation, remains a permanent commentary on human nature. The directness and precision of De Flores are masterly, as is also the virtuousness of Beatrice on first realizing his motives—

> *Why, 'tis impossible thou canst be so wicked,*
> *Or shelter such a cunning cruelty,*
> *To make his death the murderer of my honour!*
> *Thy language is so bold and vicious,*
> *I cannot see which way I can forgive it*
> *With any modesty*

—a passage which ends with the really great lines of De Flores, lines of which Shakespeare or Sophocles might have been proud:

> *Can you weep Fate from its determined purpose?*
> *So soon may you weep me.*

But what constitutes the essence of the tragedy is something which has not been sufficiently remarked; it is the *habituation* of Beatrice to her sin; it becomes no longer sin but merely custom. Such is the essence of the tragedy of *Macbeth*—the habituation to crime. And in the end Beatrice, having been so long the enforced conspirator of De Flores, becomes (and this is permanently true to human nature) more *his* partner, *his* mate, than the mate and partner of the man for the love of whom she consented to the crime. Her lover disappears not only from the scene but from her own imagination. When she says of De Flores,

> *A wondrous necessary man, my lord,*

her praise is more than half sincere; and at the end she belongs far more to De Flores—towards

whom, at the beginning, she felt strong physical
repulsion—than to her lover Alsemero. It is De
Flores, in the end, to whom she belongs as Francesca
to Paolo:

> *Beneath the stars, upon yon meteor*
> *Ever hung my fate, 'mongst things corruptible;*
> *I ne'er could pluck it from him; my loathing*
> *Was prophet to the rest, but ne'er believed.*

And De Flores's cry is perfectly sincere and in
character:

> *I loved this woman in spite of her heart;*
> *Her love I earned out of Piracquo's murder . . .*
> *Yes, and her honour's prize*
> *Was my reward; I thank life for nothing*
> *But that pleasure; it was so sweet to me,*
> *That I have drunk up all, left none behind*
> *For any man to pledge me.*

The tragedy of Beatrice is not that she has lost
Alsemero, for whose possession she played; it is
that she has won De Flores. Such tragedies are not
limited to Elizabethan times: they happen every day
and perpetually. The greatest tragedies are occupied
with great and permanent moral conflicts: the great
tragedies of Aeschylus, of Sophocles, of Corneille, of
Racine, of Shakespeare, have the same burden. In
poetry, in dramatic technique, *The Changeling* is
inferior to the best plays of Webster. But in the
moral essence of tragedy it is safe to say that in this
play Middleton is surpassed by one Elizabethan
alone, and that is Shakespeare. In some respects in

which Elizabethan tragedy can be compared to French or to Greek tragedy *The Changeling* stands above every tragic play of its time, except those of Shakespeare.

The genius which blazed in *The Changeling* was fitful but not accidental. The best tragedy after *The Changeling* is *Women Beware Women*. The thesis of the play, as the title indicates, is more arbitrary and less fundamental. The play itself, although less disfigured by ribaldry or clowning, is more tedious. Middleton sinks himself in conventional moralizing of the epoch; so that, if we are impatient, we decide that he gives merely a document of Elizabethan humbug—and then suddenly a personage will blaze out in genuine fire of vituperation. The wickedness of the personages in *Women Beware Women* is conventional wickedness of the stage of the time; yet slowly the exasperation of Bianca, the wife who married beneath her, beneath the ambitions to which she was entitled, emerges from the negative; slowly the real human passions emerge from the mesh of interest in which they begin. And here again Middleton, in writing what appears on the surface a conventional picture-palace Italian melodrama of the time, has caught permanent human feelings. And in this play Middleton shows his interest—more than any of his contemporaries—in innuendo and double meanings; and makes use of that game of chess, which he was to use more openly and directly for satire in that perfect piece of literary political art, *A Game at Chesse*. The irony could not be improved upon:

Did I not say my duke would fetch you o'er, Widow?
I think you spoke in earnest when you said it,
madam.
And my black king makes all the haste he can too.
Well, madam, we may meet with him in time yet.
I've given thee blind mate twice.

There is hardly anything truer in Elizabethan drama
than Bianca's gradual self-will and self-importance
in consequence of her courtship by the Duke:

Troth, you speak wondrous well for your old house
here;
'Twill shortly fall down at your feet to thank you,
Or stoop, when you go to bed, like a good child,
To ask you blessing.

In spite of all the long-winded speeches, in spite of
all the conventional Italianate horrors, Bianca
remains, like Beatrice in *The Changeling,* a real
woman; as real, indeed, as any woman of Elizabethan tragedy. Bianca is a type of the woman who
is purely moved by vanity.

But if Middleton understood women in tragedy
better than any of the Elizabethans—better than the
creator of the Duchess of Malfy, better than Marlowe,
better than Tourneur, or Shirley, or Fletcher, better
than any of them except Shakespeare alone—he
was also able, in his comedy, to present a finer
woman than any of them. *The Roaring Girle* has no
apparent relation to Middleton's tragedies, yet it is
agreed to be primarily the work of Middleton. It
is typical of the comedies of Middleton, and it is

the best. In his tragedies Middleton employs all the
Italianate horrors of his time, and obviously for the
purpose of pleasing the taste of his time; yet underneath we feel always a quiet and undisturbed vision
of things as they are and not "another thing." So
in his comedies. The comedies are long-winded; the
fathers are heavy fathers, and rant as heavy fathers
should; the sons are wild and wanton sons, and
perform all the pranks to be expected of them; the
machinery is the usual Elizabethan machinery;
Middleton is solicitous to please his audience with
what they expect; but there is underneath the same
steady impersonal passionless observation of human
nature. *The Roaring Girle* is as artificial as any
comedy of the time; its plot creaks loudly; yet the
Girl herself is always real. She may rant, she may
behave preposterously, but she remains a type of the
sort of woman who has renounced all happiness for
herself and who lives only for a principle. Nowhere
more than in *The Roaring Girle* can the hand of
Middleton be distinguished more clearly from the
hand of Dekker. Dekker is all sentiment; and, indeed,
in the so admired passages of *A Fair Quarrel,* exploited by Lamb, the mood if not the hand of
Dekker seems to the unexpert critic to be more
present than Middleton's. *A Fair Quarrel* seems as
much, if not more, Dekker's than Middleton's. Simi-
larly with *The Spanish Gipsie,* which can with difficulty be attributed to Middleton. But the feeling
about Moll Cut-Purse of *The Roaring Girle* is
Middleton's rather than anybody's. In Middleton's
tragedy there is a strain of realism underneath,

which is one with the poetry; and in his comedy we find the same thing.

In her recent book on *The Social Mode of Restoration Comedy,* Miss Kathleen Lynch calls attention to the gradual transition from Elizabethan-Jacobean to Restoration comedy. She observes, what is certainly true, that Middleton is the greatest "realist" in Jacobean comedy. Miss Lynch's extremely suggestive thesis is that the transition from Elizabethan-Jacobean to later Caroline comedy is primarily economic: that the interest changes from the citizen aping gentry to the citizen become gentry and accepting that code of manners. In the comedy of Middleton certainly there is as yet no code of manners; but the merchant of Cheapside is *aiming* at becoming a member of the country gentry. Miss Lynch remarks: "Middleton's keen concentration on the spectacle of the interplay of different social classes marks an important development in realistic comedy." She calls attention to this aspect of Middleton's comedy, that it marks, better than the romantic comedy of Shakespeare, or the comedy of Jonson, occupied with what Jonson thought to be permanent and not transient aspects of human nature, the transition between the aristocratic world which preceded the Tudors and the plutocratic modern world which the Tudors initiated and encouraged. By the time of the return of Charles II, as Miss Lynch points out, society had been reorganized and formed, and social conventions had been created. In the Tudor times birth still counted (though nearly all the great families were extinct); by the time of Charles II only breeding counted. The comedy of Middleton, and the comedy of Brome, and the comedy of Shirley, is intermediate, as Miss Lynch remarks. Middleton, she observes, marks the transitional stage in which the London tradesman was anxious to cease to be a tradesman and to become a country gentleman. The words of his City Magnate in *Michaelmas Terme* have not yet lost their point:

"A fine journey in the Whitsun holydays, i'faith, to ride with a number of cittizens and their wives, some upon pillions, some upon side-saddles, I and little Thomasine i' the middle, our son and heir, Sim Quomodo, in a peach-colour taffeta jacket, some horse length, or a long yard before us—there will be a fine show on's I can tell you."

But Middleton's comedy is not, like the comedy of Congreve, the comedy of a set social behaviour; it is still, like the later comedy of Dickens, the comedy of individuals, in spite of the continual motions of city merchants towards county gentility. In the comedy of the Restoration a figure such as that of Moll Cut-Purse would have been impossible. As a social document the comedy of Middleton illustrates the transition from government by a landed aristocracy to government by a city aristocracy gradually engrossing the land. As such it is of the greatest interest. But as literature, as a dispassionate picture of human nature, Middleton's comedy deserves to be remembered chiefly by its real—perpetually real—and human figure of Moll the Roaring Girl. That Middleton's comedy was "photographic," that it

introduces us to the low life of the time far
better than anything in the comedy of Shakespeare
or the comedy of Jonson, better than anything
except the pamphlets of Dekker and Greene and
Nashe, there is little doubt. But it produced one
great play—*The Roaring Girle*—a great play in
spite of the tedious long speeches of some of the
principal characters, in spite of the clumsy machinery
of the plot: for the reason that Middleton was a
great observer of human nature, without fear, without sentiment, without prejudice.

And Middleton in the end—after criticism has
subtracted all that Rowley, all that Dekker, all that
others contributed—is a great example of great
English drama. He has no message; he is merely a
great recorder. Incidentally, in flashes and when
the dramatic need comes, he is a great poet, a
great master of versification:

> *I that am of your blood was taken from you*
> *For your better health; look no more upon 't,*
> *But cast it to the ground regardlessly,*
> *Let the common sewer take it from distinction:*
> *Beneath the stars, upon yon meteor*
> *Ever hung my fate, 'mongst things corruptible;*
> *I ne'er could pluck it from him; my loathing*
> *Was prophet to the rest, but ne'er believed.*

The man who wrote these lines remains inscrutable,
solitary, unadmired; welcoming collaboration, indifferent to fame; dying no one knows when and no
one knows how; attracting, in three hundred years,
no personal admiration. Yet he wrote one tragedy

which more than any play except those of Shake-speare has a profound and permanent moral value and horror; and one comedy which more than any Elizabethan comedy realizes a free and noble woman-hood.

Thomas Heywood

There are a few of the Elizabethan dramatists, notably Marlowe and Ben Jonson, who always return to our minds with the reality of personal acquaintances. We know them unmistakably through their own writings—Jonson partly through his conversations with Drummond—and by a few anecdotes of the kind which, even when apocryphal, remain as evidence of the personal impression that such men must have made upon their contemporaries. There are others whom we can remember only by the association of their names with a play, or a group of plays. Of all these men Thomas Heywood is one of the dimmest figures; and it is interesting to remark how very dim he still remains even after Dr. Clark's exhaustive industry.[1] Dr. Clark appears to have discovered and assembled all the information that we can ever expect to have; and it is certainly not his fault that Heywood makes still but a faint impression; in fact, Dr. Clark's book can help us considerably to understand why this is so. The book

[1] *Thomas Heywood: Playwright and Miscellanist,* by A. M. Clark (Oxford: Blackwell, 1931).

is solidly documentary; it is not, like some biographical essays with scanty material, stuffed out with appreciation and conjecture. It is, in fact, an admirable account of the life of a typical literary jack-of-all-trades of the epoch; the summary of Heywood's activities as a pamphleteer, with his works of what may be termed popular theology in the Puritan cause, is full of interest for any one who cares about this lively and, in some respects, very remote age. And the book confirms the impression that Heywood —whom Dr. Clark shows convincingly to have been a Heywood of Mottram, in Cheshire, and not of *the* family of Heywood of Lincolnshire, the county of his birth—was a facile and sometimes felicitous purveyor of goods to the popular taste.

Heywood's reputation, which we owe primarily to Lamb and Hazlitt, is founded on *A Woman Killed with Kindness;* but *The English Traveller* and *The Wise-Woman of Hogsdon* are not far below it; and the first part of *The Fair Maid of the West,* when it has been performed—twice, we believe, in recent years—was revealed as a rollicking piece of popular patriotic sentiment. Before considering whether this output has enough coherence to be treated with the dignity of an *œuvre,* there are several interesting attributions of Dr. Clark's which demand attention. The first and most important is *Appius and Virginia.*

The date of this play, which has long been a difficulty to students of Webster—a play far below Webster's best work, and in some respects dissimilar to it—forms one of Dr. Clark's reasons for attribut-

ing the play primarily to Heywood. This was, of
course, the guess of Rupert Brooke; but, given the
initial doubt which strikes any admirer of Webster,
the opinion, when it comes from a close student of
Heywood, has much stronger authority. Dr. Clark,
however, is not content to take issue only with Mr.
Sykes (who gives the whole play to Webster), though
that is a serious task in itself. He dismisses, with
hardly more attention than a few footnotes, the
moderate and so far, we believe, impregnable view
of Mr. F. L. Lucas. He refers, certainly, to Mr.
Lucas's "attempt to depreciate Heywood" as "un-
critical"; because Mr. Lucas, in his introduction to
the play in his complete edition of Webster, doubts
whether Heywood

"could have produced unaided so well-planned and
reasonable a play. For there is a peculiar oafish
simplicity about him which made him unable ever
to create a single piece, except perhaps *Edward IV,*
which is not deformed by pages of utter drivel."

Mr. Lucas has perhaps written with a heat uncommon among Elizabethan scholars, though refresh-
ing; yet his doubt whether Heywood could have
planned the play is one likely to strike any one who
reads both Webster and Heywood without prej-
udices. To such a reader, the fact that Heywood
is the author of *The Rape of Lucrece* strains cre-
dulity to the breaking point. But this, indeed, is
the whole issue between Dr. Clark and Mr. Lucas.
Neither doubts that both Heywood and Webster had
a hand in the play; neither makes a claim for any

third author. Dr. Clark concludes that Heywood
wrote the play and that "at an unknown date
Webster revised the play somewhat carelessly." Mr.
Lucas can more easily believe that Webster wrote,
or designed and partly wrote, the play, and that
Heywood either revised or completed it. We are
left with a narrow choice and a fine distinction;
in fact, we are left to our personal impressions. The
feeling of the present reviewer, at least, is that the
structure of the play is more credibly assignable to
Webster, as well as the good lines which nobody
denies him.

Our inclination to this conclusion is confirmed,
if anything, by Dr. Clark's theory of Heywood's
hand in *The Jew of Malta*. It seems to us that here
Dr. Clark's scholarly theory is really founded upon
a critical presupposition. He holds a not uncommon
view that "so far as [Marlowe's] conception of
Barabas is concerned, the play might finish with the
second act." But he adds, "so far as we know Marlowe
invented the plot," which is a considerable conces-
sion; and also admits that there is a very little in
Acts iii, iv, and v which Marlowe may have written.
He says, "in the play we probably still have the main
incidents as originally determined, but now crowded
mostly into v to make room for certain ribaldry and
gruesome farce." There is perhaps a little ribaldry
which we should prefer not to attribute to Marlowe,
and of a kind of which Heywood was certainly
capable; but the most "gruesome farce" is found in
Act iv, Scenes i and ii; which the mere critic may
maintain to be farce of a gruesomeness a cut above

Heywood, and by no means unworthy of Marlowe. That the latter part of the play is garbled, few would doubt; that the writer who filled in the remains of Marlowe's play was Heywood, Dr. Clark makes out a good case; but mutilated and patched as the play probably is, we may still see in it a conception of Barabas which is by no means finished with the second act.

The third of Dr. Clark's interesting ascriptions concerns *A Yorkshire Tragedy*. This abrupt little play has been somewhat overrated, singularly so by Swinburne. Dr. Clark's association of it with *The Miseries of Enforced Marriage,* and his explanation of its inconsistencies through this association, is an excellent piece of reasoning. So far as the verse is concerned, the most of it is not too bad to be Heywood's, and the best line and a half—

> *But you are playing in the angels' laps*
> *And will not look on me—*

strike us as a *trouvaille* which might have been possible to Heywood. The best of the play is the part of the "little son":

"What, ail you, father? are you not well? I cannot scourge my top as long as you stand so: you take up all the room with your wide legs. Puh, you cannot make me afeard with this; I fear no vizards, nor bugbears"—

and as we cannot allege any other minor dramatist as more competent to have written this touching dialogue than Heywood, we are hardly in a strong position to refuse it to him. This then, we think, is the most valuable of Dr. Clark's ascriptions.

None of these attributions, interesting as is the last of them in itself, can make very much difference to our estimate of Heywood as a dramatist and a poet; and it is upon the indisputable plays that we found our opinion of him. These indisputable plays exhibit what may be called the minimum degree of unity. Similar subject-matter and treatment appear in several; the same stage skill, the same versifying ability. The sensibility is merely that of ordinary people in ordinary life—which is the reason, perhaps, why Heywood is misleadingly called a "realist." Behind the motions of his personages, the shadows of the human world, there is no reality of moral synthesis; to inform the verse there is no vision, none of the artist's power to give undefinable unity to the most various material. In the work of nearly all of those of his contemporaries who are as well known as he there is at least some inchoate pattern: there is, as it would often be called, personality. Of those of Heywood's plays which are worth reading, each is worth reading for itself, but none throws any illumination upon any other.

Heywood's versification is never on a very high poetic level, but at its best is often on a high dramatic level. This can be illustrated by one of the best known of quotations from *A Woman Killed with Kindness:*

O speak no more!
For more than this I know, and have recorded
Within the red-leaved table of my heart.

Fair, and of all beloved, I was not fearful
Bluntly to give my life into your hand,
And at one hazard all my earthly means.
Go, tell your husband; he will turn me off,
And I am then undone. I care not, I;
'Twas for your sake. Perchance in rage he'll kill me,
I care not, 'twas for you. Say I incur
The general name of villain through the world,
Of traitor to my friend; I care not, I.
Beggary, shame, death, scandal, and reproach,
For you I'll hazard all: why, what care I?
For you I'll live, and in your love I'll die.

The image at the beginning of this passage does not, it is true, deserve its fame. "Table of my heart" is a legitimate, though hardly striking, metaphor; but to call it *red-leaved* is to press the anatomical aspect into a ridiculous figure. It is not a conceit, as when Crashaw deliberately telescopes one image into another, but merely the irreflective grasping after a fine trope. But in the lines that follow the most skilful use is made of regular blank verse to emphasize the argument; and it is, even to the judicious couplet at the end, a speech which any actor should be happy to declaim. The speech is perfect for the situation; the most persuasive that Wendoll could have made to Mrs. Frankford; and it persuades us into accepting her surrender. And this instance of verse which is only moderately poetical but very highly dramatic is by no means singular in Heywood's work.

And undeniably Heywood was not without skill

in the construction of plays. It is unreasonable to complain of *A Woman Killed with Kindness* that it is improbable that a woman who has lived very happily with her husband and borne children should suddenly and easily be seduced by a man who had been living in the house the whole time; we consider that the seduction is made extremely plausible. What is perhaps clumsy is the beginning superfluously by a scene directly after the marriage of the Frankfords, instead of by a scene marking the happiness of the pair up to the moment of Wendoll's declaration. Sufficient verisimilitude is maintained to the end; we accept the Elizabethan convention of very quick death from heartbreak; and the last scene is really affecting. It is true that Mistress Frankford's words:

Out of my zeal to Heaven, whither now I'm bound,

seem to rely upon some curiously unorthodox theology; and even if death from broken heart secures the remission of sins, it hardly became Mrs. Frankford to be so certain of it. But such a moral sentiment is perhaps not unique in the ethics of Elizabethan drama; and other small touches in the play, such as the finding of the guitar, well deserve the praise they have received. It is in the underplot, as in some other plays, that Heywood is least skilful. This theme—a man ready to prostitute his sister as payment for a debt of honour—is too grotesque even to horrify us; but it is too obviously there merely because an underplot is required to fill out the play for us to feel anything but boredom when it recurs.

Middleton's *The Changeling,* in every other respect
a far finer play, must share with *A Woman Killed
with Kindness* the discredit of having the weakest
underplot of any important play in the whole Elizabethan repertory.

Indeed, Heywood suffers from one great handicap
in attempting to write underplots at all—he was
gifted with very little sense of humour, and therefore
could not fall back upon the comic for the purpose.
In attempting to be amusing he sometimes has
recourse, as other men than harried playwrights
have been known to do, to the lowest bawdiness,
which leaves us less with a sense of repugnance for
the man who could write it than with a sense of
pity for the man who could think of nothing better.
Here and there, in *The Wise-Woman of Hogsdon*
for instance, he succeeds with something not too far
below Jonson to be comparable to that master's
work; the wise woman herself, and her scenes with
her clientele, are capitally done, and earn for
Heywood the title of "realist" if any part of his
work can. The scene of the unmasking of Young
Chartley must be excellent fun when played. The
underplot of *The English Traveller,* on the other
hand, is a clumsy failure to do that in which only
Jonson could have succeeded. But Heywood has no
imaginative humour; and as he has so often been
spoken of in the same breath with Dekker, that is
a comparison which may justly be made. Just as
Bess, the Fair Maid of the West, is a purely melo-
dramatic figure beside the heroine of *The Roaring
Girle,* so Heywood could no more have created the

character of Cuddie Banks, in *The Witch,* than he could have written the magnificent tirade (a tirade which, if anything can, goes to prove that Middleton wrote *The Revenger's Tragedy*) which Middleton puts into the mouth of the chief character in the same play. Cuddie Banks, loving the dog whom he knows to be a devil, but loving him as dog while reproving him as devil, is worthy to rank with clowns of Shakespeare; he is not "realistic," he is true.

It was in *The English Traveller* that Heywood found his best plot. Possibly the elder critics disapproved of the heroine's plighting herself to marry her admirer as soon as her elderly husband should die; but it is far less offensive to modern taste than many other situations in Elizabethan drama, and it is one which a modern novelist—not perhaps a quite modern novelist, but a Stendhal—might have made the most of. It is indeed a plot especially modern among Elizabethan plots; for the refinement of agony of the virtuous lover who has controlled his passion and then discovers that his lady has deceived both her husband, who is his friend, and himself, is really more poignant than the torment of the betrayed husband Frankford. The strange situation *à quatre,* Master Wincott and his wife, young Geraldine and his faithless companion Delavil—and old Geraldine neatly worked into the pattern as well—is not only well thought of but well thought out; and it is delicately phrased:

Y. GER.

> *Your husband's old, to whom my soul doth wish*
> *A Nestor's age, so much he merits from me;*

> *Yet if (as proof and Nature daily teach*
> *Men cannot always live, especially*
> *Such as are old and crazed) he be called hence,*
> *Fairly, in full maturity of time,*
> *And we two be reserved to after-life,*
> *Will you confer your widowhood on me?*

WIFE.

> *You ask the thing I was about to beg;*
> *Your tongue hath spoke mine own thoughts. . . .*

WIFE.

> *Till that day come, you shall reserve yourself*
> *A single man; converse nor company*
> *With any woman, contract nor combine*
> *With maid or widow; which expected hour*
> *As I do wish not haste, so when it happens*
> *It shall not come unwelcome. You hear all;*
> *Vow this.*

Y. GER.

> *By all that you have said, I swear,*
> *And by this kiss confirm.*

WIFE.

> *You're now my brother;*
> *But then, my second husband.*

It could not have been done better. As in the passage
from *A Woman Killed with Kindness* quoted above,
the verse, which nowhere bursts into a flame of
poetry, is yet economical and tidy, and formed to
extract all the dramatic value possible from the situation. And it is by his refinement of sentiment, by

his sympathetic delicacy in these two plays, that Heywood deserves, and well deserves, to be remembered; for here he has accomplished what none of his contemporaries succeeded in accomplishing.

Yet we must concede that the interest is always sentimental, and never ethical. One has seen plays in our time which are just the sort of thing that Heywood would have written had he been our contemporary. It is usual for inferior authors at any time to accept whatever morality is current, because they are interested not to analyse the ethics but to exploit the sentiment. Mrs. Frankford yields to her seducer with hardly a struggle, and her decline and death are a tribute to popular sentiment; not, certainly, a vindication of inexorable moral law. She is in the sentimental tradition which peopled a period of nineteenth-century fiction with Little Em'lys; and which, if it now produces a generation of rather robuster heroines, has yet made no moral advance, because it has no vital relation to morals at all. For a Corneille or a Racine, the centre of interest in the situation of Mrs. Frankford or Mrs. Wincott would have been the moral conflict leading up to the fall; and even the absence of conflict, as in the seduction of Mathilde (if seduction it can be called) in *Le Rouge et le Noir,* can be treated by a moralist. The capital distinction is that between representation of human actions which have moral reality and representation of such as have only sentimental reality; and besides this, any distinction between "healthy" and "morbid" sentiment is trivial. It is well enough to speak of Heywood, as does Dr.

Clark, as "a man of tender charity . . . ever kindly
to the fallen and with a gift of homely pathos and
simple poetry"; though it does less than justice to
Heywood to describe his pathos as "homely" (for the
famous pathos of "Nan, Nan!" is no homelier than
Lear's "Never, never, never, never, never," though
far below it). What matters is not whether Heywood
was inspired by tender charity, but whether his
actual productions are any more edifying, any more
moral, than what Dr. Clark would call "the slippery
ethics" of Fletcher, Massinger, and Ford.

The ethics of most of the greater Elizabethan
dramatists is only intelligible as leading up to, or
deriving from, that of Shakespeare: it has its significance, we mean, only in the light of Shakespeare's
fuller revelation. There is another type of ethics, that
of the satirist. In Shakespeare's work it is represented
most nearly by *Timon* and *Troilus,* but in a mind
with such prodigious capacity of development as
Shakespeare's, the snarling vein could not endure.
The kind of satire which is approached in *The Jew
of Malta* reaches perhaps its highest point with *Volpone;* but it is a kind to which also approximates
much of the work of Middleton and Tourneur, men
who as writers must be counted morally higher than
Fletcher, Ford, or Heywood.

These by enchantments can whole lordships change
To trunks of rich attire, turn ploughs and teams
To Flanders mares and coaches, and huge trains
Of servitors to a French butterfly.
Have you not city-witches who can turn

Their husbands' wares, whole standing shops of wares,
To sumptuous tables, gardens of stolen sin;
In one year wasting what scarce twenty win?
Are not these witches?

That dolorous aspect of human nature which in comedy is best portrayed by Molière, though Jonson and even Wycherley have the same burden, appears again and again in the tragic drama of Middleton and Tourneur. Without denying to Heywood what Dr. Clark attributes to him, a sense of "the pity of it," we can find a profounder sense of the "pity of it" in the lines quoted above which Middleton gives to the Witch of Edmonton. Heywood's sense of pity is genuine enough, but it is only the kind of pity that the ordinary playgoer, of any time, can appreciate. Heywood's is a drama of common life, not, in the highest sense, tragedy at all; there is no supernatural music from behind the wings. He would in any age have been a successful playwright; he is eminent in the pathetic, rather than the tragic. His nearest approach to those deeper emotions which shake the veil of Time is in that fine speech of Frankford which surely no man or woman past youth can read without a twinge of personal feeling:

O God! O God! that it were possible
To undo things done; to call back yesterday. . . .

Cyril Tourneur

Although the tragedies which make immortal the name of Cyril Tourneur are accessible to every one in the Mermaid edition, it is still an event to have a new edition of the "work" of this strange poet. Fifty-two years have passed since the edition in two volumes by Churton Collins. And this sumptuous critical edition of Professor Nicoll's[1] reminds us that it is time to revalue the work of Tourneur.

None of the Elizabethan dramatists is more puzzling; none offers less foothold for the scholarly investigator; and none is more dangerous for the literary critic. We know almost nothing of his life; we trace his hand in no collaboration. He has left only two plays; and it has been doubted even whether the same man wrote both; and if he did, as most scholars agree, there is still some doubt as to which he wrote first. Yet in no plays by any minor Elizabethan is a more positive personality revealed than in *The Revenger's Tragedy*. No Elizabethan

[1] *The Works of Cyril Tourneur,* edited by Allardyce Nicoll, with decorations by Frederick Carter (London: The Fanfrolico Press).

dramatist offers greater temptation: to the scholar, to
hazard conjecture of fact; and to the critic, to hazard
conjecture of significance. We may be sure that what
Mr. Nicoll does not know is unknown to anybody;
and it is no disrespect to his scholarship and dili-
gence to remark how little, in the fifty-two years of
Elizabethan research since Collins, has been added to
our knowledge of the singular poet with the de-
lightful name. Churton Collins, in his admirable
introduction, really knows nothing at all about the
man's life; and all that later students have been able
to do is to piece together several probable shreds.
That there was a family of Tourneurs is certain; the
precise place in it of Cyril is, as Mr. Nicoll freely
admits, a matter of speculation. And with all the
plausible guesses possible, Mr. Nicoll tells us that
Tourneur's "whole early life is a complete blank."
What he does give us is good reason for believing
that Tourneur, with perhaps other members of the
family, was a servant of the Cecils; and he adds to
our knowledge a prose piece, "The Character of
Robert Earl of Salisbury." Besides the two tragedies,
he also gives "The Transformed Metamorphosis,"
the "Funeral Poem upon the Death of Sir Francis
Vere," and the Elegy on the death of Prince Henry,
already canonically attributed to Tourneur; and
"Laugh and Lie Down," a satirical pamphlet, no
better and no worse than dozens of others, which is
probably Tourneur's—at least, it is attributed to him,
and there is no particular reason why he should not
be the author.

The information of fifty years is meagre, and prob-

ably will never be improved. It is astonishingly in-
congruous with what we feel we know about Tourneur after reading the two plays: two plays as different from all plays by known Elizabethans as they
are from each other. In Elizabethan drama, the critic
is rash who will assert boldly that any play is by a
single hand. But with each of these, *The Atheist's
Tragedy* and *The Revenger's Tragedy,* the literary
critic feels that, even were there some collaboration,
one mind guided the whole work; and feels that the
mind was not that of one of the other well-known
dramatic writers. Certainly, Tourneur has made a
very deep impression upon the minds of those critics
who have admired him. It is to be regretted, however, that Professor Nicoll, at the beginning of his
otherwise sober and just introduction, has quoted
the hysterical phrase of Marcel Schwob's *vie imagi-
naire* of Tourneur. To say that Tourneur *naquit de
l'union d'un dieu inconnu avec une prostituée* is a
pardonable excess of a romantic period, a pardonable excess on the part of a poet discovering a foreign poet. But this is not criticism; and it is a misleading introduction to the work of a man who was
a great English poet; and it produces an impression
which is increased by the excellent but too *macabre*
decorations of Mr. Carter. What matters first is the
beauty of the verse and the unity of the dramatic
pattern in the two plays.

The author of *The Atheist's Tragedy* and *The
Revenger's Tragedy* belongs critically among the earlier of the followers of Shakespeare. If Ford and Shirley
and Fletcher represent the decadence, and Webster

the last ripeness, then Tourneur belongs a little earlier than Webster. He is nearer to Middleton, and has some affinity to that curious and still underestimated poet Marston. The difference between his mind and that of Webster is very great; if we assigned his plays to any other known dramatist, Webster would be the last choice. For Webster is a slow, deliberate, careful writer, very much the conscious artist. He was incapable of writing so badly or so tastelessly as Tourneur sometimes did, but he is never quite so surprising as Tourneur sometimes is. Moreover, Webster, in his greatest tragedies, has a kind of pity for *all* of his characters, an attitude towards good and bad alike which helps to unify the Webster pattern. Tourneur has no such feeling for any of his characters; and in this respect is nearer, as Professor Stoll has pointed out and Professor Nicoll has reminded us, to the author of *Antonio and Mellida*. Of all his other contemporaries, Middleton is the nearest. But Mr. Nicoll, we think quite rightly, rejects Mr. E. H. C. Oliphant's theory that Middleton is the author of *The Revenger's Tragedy,* and with Mr. Dugdale Sykes restores the play to Tourneur. And in spite of Mr. Oliphant's weight of probabilities, there is one quality of Middleton which we do not find in the two plays attributed to Tourneur. The finest of the tragic characters of Middleton live in a way which differs from Tourneur's, not in degree but kind; and they have flashes of a kind of satiric wit unknown to Tourneur, in whom wit is supplied by a fierce grotesquerie. In reading one play of Middleton, either *The Changeling* or *Women*

Beware Women, for instance, we can recognize an author capable of considerable variety in his dramatic work; in reading either of Tourneur's plays we recognize a narrow mind, capable at most of the limited range of Marston.

Indeed, none of the characters of Tourneur, even the notable Vindice, the protagonist of *The Revenger's Tragedy,* is by himself invested with much humanity either for good or evil. But dramatic characters may live in more than one way; and a dramatist like Tourneur can compensate his defects by the intensity of his virtues. Characters should be real in relation to our own life, certainly, as even a very minor character of Shakespeare may be real; but they must also be real in relation to each other; and the closeness of emotional pattern in the latter way is an important part of dramatic merit. The personages of Tourneur have, like those of Marston, and perhaps in a higher degree, this togetherness. They may be distortions, grotesques, almost childish caricatures of humanity, but they are all distorted to scale. Hence the whole action, from their appearance to their ending, "no common action" indeed, has its own self-subsistent reality. For closeness of texture, in fact, there are no plays beyond Shakespeare's, and the best of Marlowe and Jonson, that can surpass *The Revenger's Tragedy.* Tourneur excels in three virtues of the dramatist: he knew how, in his own way, to construct a plot, he was cunning in his manipulation of stage effects, and he was a master of versification and choice of language. *The Revenger's Tragedy* starts off at top speed, as every critic has observed; and never slackens to the end. We are told everything we need to know before the first scene is half over; Tourneur employs his torrent of words with the greatest economy. The opening scene and the famous Scene v of Act III are remarkable feats of melodrama; and the suddenness of the end of the final scene of Act v matches the sudden explosiveness of the beginning.

Before considering the detail of the two plays, we must face two problems which have never been solved and probably never will be: whether the two plays are by the same hand and, if so, in which order they were written. For the first point, the consensus of scholarship, with the exception of Mr. Oliphant's brilliant ascription of *The Revenger's Tragedy* to Middleton—an ascription which leaves the other play more of a mystery than before—assigns the two plays to Tourneur. For the second point, the consensus of scholarship is counter to the first impressions of sensibility; for all existing evidence points to the priority of *The Revenger's Tragedy* in time. The records of Stationer's Hall cannot be lightly disregarded; and Mr. Dugdale Sykes, who is perhaps our greatest authority on the texts of Tourneur and Middleton, finds stylistic evidence also. Professor Nicoll accepts the evidence, although pointing out clearly enough the anomaly. Certainly, any testimony drawn from the analogy of a modern poet's experience would urge that *The Athiest's Tragedy* was immature work, and that *The Revenger's Tragedy* represented a period of full mastery of blank verse. It is not merely that the latter play is in every way the

better; but that it shows a highly original development of vocabulary and metric, unlike that of every
other play and every other dramatist. The versification of *The Revenger's Tragedy* is of a very high
order indeed. And yet, with the evidence before us,
summed up briefly in Mr. Nicoll's preface, we cannot
affirm that this is the later play. Among all the
curiosities of that curious period, when dramatic
poets worked and developed in ways alien to the
modern mind, this is one of the most curious. But it
is quite possible. We may conjecture either that *The
Atheist's Tragedy* was composed, or partly composed,
and laid by until after *The Revenger's Tragedy* was
written and entered. Or that after exhausting his
best inspiration on the latter play—which certainly
bears every internal evidence of having been written
straight off in one sudden heat—Tourneur, years
after, in colder blood, with more attention to successful models—not only Shakespeare but also perhaps Chapman—produced *The Atheist's Tragedy,*
with more regular verse, more conventional moralizing, more conventional scenes, but with here and
there flashes of the old fire. Not that the scenes of
The Atheist's Tragedy are altogether conventional;
or, at least, he trespasses beyond the convention in a
personal way. There was nothing remarkable in
setting a graveyard scene at midnight; but we feel
that to set it for the action of a low assignation and
an attempted rape at the same time seems more to
be expected of the author of *The Revenger's Tragedy*
than of any one else; while the low comedy, more
low than comic, does not seem of the taste of either.

Webster or Middleton. Webster's farcical prose is
harmonious with his tragic verse; and in this respect
Webster is a worthy follower of the tradition of the
Porter in *Macbeth*. Middleton again, in his tragedies,
has a different feel of the relation of the tragic and
the comic; whereas the transitions in the two tragedies of Tourneur—and especially in *The Atheist's
Tragedy*—are exactly what one would expect from
a follower of Marston; especially in *The Atheist's
Tragedy* they have that offensive tastelessness which
is so positive as to be itself a kind of taste, which
we find in the work of Marston.

The Atheist's Tragedy is indeed a peculiar brew of
styles. It has well-known passages like the following:[2]

*Walking next day upon the fatal shore,
Among the slaughtered bodies of their men,
Which the full-stomached sea had cast upon
The sands, it was my unhappy chance to light
Upon a face, whose favour when it lived
My astonished mind informed me I had seen.
He lay in his armour, as if that had been
His coffin; and the weeping sea (like one
Whose milder temper doth lament the death
Of him whom in his rage he slew) runs up
The shore, embraces him, kisses his cheek;
Goes back again, and forces up the sands
To bury him, and every time it parts
Sheds tears upon him, till, at last (as if*

[2] The text used in the following quotations is the critical
text of Professor Nicoll; but for convenience and familiarity
the modernized spelling and punctuation of the "Mermaid"
text is used.

It could no longer endure to see the man
Whom it had slain, yet loth to leave him) with
A kind of unresolved unwilling pace,
Winding her waves one in another, (like
A man that folds his arms, or wrings his hands
For grief) ebbed from the body, and descends;
As if it would sink down into the earth
And hide itself for shame of such a deed.

The present writer was once convinced that *The Atheist's Tragedy* was the earlier play. But lines like these, masterly but artificial, might well belong to a later period; the regularity of the versification, the elaboration of the long suspended sentences, with three similes expressed in brackets, remind us even of Massinger. It is true that Charles Lamb, commenting on this passage, refers this parenthetical style to Sir Philip Sidney, who "seems to have set the example to Shakespeare"; but these lines have closer syntactical parallels in Massinger than in Shakespeare. But lines like

To spend our substance on a minute's pleasure

remind one of *The Revenger's Tragedy,* and lines like

Your gravity becomes your perished soul
As hoary mouldiness does rotten fruit

of *The Revenger's Tragedy* where it is likest Middleton.

As a parallel for admitting the possibility of *The Atheist's Tragedy* being the later play, Professor

Nicoll cites the fact that *Cymbeline* is later than *Hamlet*. This strikes us as about the most unsuitable parallel that could be found. Even though some critics may still consider *Cymbeline* as evidence of "declining powers," it has no less a mastery of words than *Hamlet,* and possibly more; and, like every one of Shakespeare's plays, it adds something or develops something not explicit in any previous play, it has its place in an orderly sequence. Now accepting the canonical order of Tourneur's two plays, *The Atheist's Tragedy* adds nothing at all to what the other play has given us; there is no development, no fresh inspiration; only the skilful but uninspired use of a greater metrical variety. Cases are not altogether wanting, among poets, of a precocious maturity exceeding the limits of the poet's experience— in contrast to the very slow and very long development of Shakespeare—a maturity to which the poet is never again able to catch up. Tourneur's genius, in any case, is in *The Revenger's Tragedy;* his talent only in *The Atheist's Tragedy.*

Indeed, *The Revenger's Tragedy* might well be a specimen of such isolated masterpieces. It does express—and this, chiefly, is what gives it its amazing unity—an intense and unique and horrible vision of life; but is such a vision as might come, as the result of few or slender experiences, to a highly sensitive adolescent with a gift for words. We are apt to expect of youth only a fragmentary view of life; we incline to see youth as exaggerating the importance of its narrow experience and imagining the world as did Chicken Licken. But occasionally the intensity of the vision of its own ecstasies or horrors, combined with a mastery of word and rhythm, may give to a juvenile work a universality which is beyond the author's knowledge of life to give, and to which mature men and women can respond. Churton Collins' introduction to the works is by far the most penetrating interpretation of Tourneur that has been written; and this introduction, though Collins believed *The Revenger's Tragedy* to be the later play, and although he thinks of Tourneur as a man of mature experience, does not invalidate this theory. "Tourneur's great defect as a dramatic poet," says Collins, "is undoubtedly the narrowness of his range of vision": and this narrowness of range might be that of a young man. The cynicism, the loathing and disgust of humanity, expressed consummately in *The Revenger's Tragedy*, are immature in the respect that they exceed the object. Their objective equivalents are characters practising the grossest vices; characters which seem merely to be spectres projected from the poet's inner world of nightmare, some horror beyond words. So the play is a document on humanity chiefly because it is a document on one human being, Tourneur; its motive is truly the death motive, for it is the loathing and horror of life itself. To have realized this motive so well is a triumph; for the hatred of life is an important phase—even, if you like, a mystical experience—in life itself.

The Revenger's Tragedy, then, is in this respect quite different from any play by any minor Elizabethan; it can, in this respect, be compared only to

Hamlet. Perhaps, however, its quality would be better marked by contrasting it with a later work of cynicism and loathing, *Gulliver's Travels.* No two compositions could be more dissimilar. Tourneur's "Suffering, cynicism and despair," to use Collins' words, are static; they might be prior to experience, or be the fruit of but little; Swift's is the progressive cynicism of the mature and disappointed man of the world. As an objective comment on the world, Swift's is by far the more terrible. For Swift had himself enough pettiness, as well as enough sin of pride, and lust of dominion, to be able to expose and condemn mankind by its universal pettiness and pride and vanity and ambition; and his poetry, as well as his prose, attests that he hated the very smell of the human animal. We may think as we read Swift, "how loathesome human beings are"; in reading Tourneur we can only think, "how terrible to loathe human beings so much as that." For you cannot make humanity horrible merely by presenting human beings as consistent and monotonous maniacs of gluttony and lust.

Collins, we think, tended to read into the plays of Tourneur too much, or more than is necessary, of a lifetime's experience. Some of his phrases, however, are memorable and just. But what still remains to be praised, after Swinburne and Collins and Mr. Nicoll, is Tourneur's unique style in blank verse. His occasional verses are mediocre at best; he left no lyric verse at all; but it is hardly too much to say that, after Marlowe, Shakespeare, and Webster, Tourneur is the most remakable technical innovator—an

innovator who found no imitators. The style of *The
Revenger's Tragedy* is consistent throughout; there is
little variation, but the rapidity escapes monotony.

*Faith, if the truth were known, I was begot
After some gluttonous dinner; some stirring dish
Was my first father, when deep healths went round
And ladies' cheeks were painted red with wine,
Their tongues, as short and nimble as their heels,
Uttering words sweet and thick; and when they rose,
Were merrily disposed to fall again.
In such a whispering and withdrawing hour . . .
                                . . . and, in the morning
When they are up and drest, and their mask on,
Who can perceive this, save that eternal eye
That sees through flesh and all? Well, if anything be
       damned,
It will be twelve o'clock at night. . . .*

His verse hurries:

*O think upon the pleasure of the palace!
Secured ease and state! the stirring meats,
Ready to move out of the dishes, that e'en now
Quicken when they are eaten!
Banquets abroad by torchlight! music! sports!
Bareheaded vassals, that had ne'er the fortune
To keep on their own hats, but let horns wear 'em!
Nine coaches waiting—hurry, hurry, hurry—*

His phrases seem to contract the images in his effort
to say everything in the least space, the shortest time:

> *Age and bare bone*
> *Are e'er allied in action . . .*

To suffer wet damnation to run through 'em . . .

The poor benefit of a bewildering minute . . .

(*Bewildering* is the reading of the Mermaid text; both Churton Collins and Mr. Nicoll give *bewitching* without mentioning any alternative reading: it is a pity if they be right, for *bewildering* is much the richer word here.)

> *forgetful feasts . . .*

> *falsify highways . . .*

And the peculiar abruptness, the frequent change of tempo, characteristic of *The Revenger's Tragedy,* is nowhere better shown than by the closing lines:

This murder might have slept in tongueless brass,
But for ourselves, and the world died an ass.
Now I remember too, here was Piato
Brought forth a knavish sentence once;
No doubt (said he), but time
Will make the murderer bring forth himself.
'Tis well he died; he was a witch.
And now, my lord, since we are in forever,
This work was ours, which else might have been
*   slipped!*
And if we list, we could have nobles clipped,
And go for less than beggars; but we hate
To bleed so cowardly, we have enough,

I' faith, we're well, our mother turned, our sister true,
We die after a nest of dukes. Adieu!

The versification, as indeed the whole style of *The Revenger's Tragedy,* is not that of the last period of the great drama. Although so peculiar, the metric of Tourneur is earlier in style than that of the later Shakespeare, or Fletcher, or Webster, to say nothing of Massinger, or Shirley, or Ford. It seems to derive, as much as from any one's, from that of Marston. What gives Tourneur his place as a great poet is this one play, in which a horror of life, singular in his own or any age, finds exactly the right words and the right rhythms.

John Ford

Among other possible classifications, we might divide
the Elizabethan and Jacobean dramatists into those
who would have been great even had Shakespeare
never lived, those who are positive enough to have
brought some positive contribution after Shakespeare,
and those whose merit consists merely in having exploited successfully a few Shakespearean devices or
echoed here and there the Shakespearean verse. In
the first class would fall Marlowe, Jonson, and Chapman; in the second, Middleton, Webster, and Tourneur; in the third, Beaumont and Fletcher and
Shirley as tragedian. This kind of division could not
support very close question, especially in its distinction between the second and the third class; but
it is of some use at the beginning, in helping us to
assign a provisional place to John Ford.

The standard set by Shakespeare is that of a continuous development from first to last, a development in which the choice both of theme and of
dramatic and verse technique in each play seems to
be determined increasingly by Shakespeare's state of
feeling, by the particular stage of his emotional ma-

turity at the time. What is "the whole man" is not
simply his greatest or maturest achievement, but the
whole pattern formed by the sequence of plays; so
that we may say confidently that the full meaning
of any one of his plays is not in itself alone, but in
that play in the order in which it was written, in its
relation to all of Shakespeare's other plays, earlier
and later: we must know all of Shakespeare's work
in order to know any of it. No other dramatist of
the time approaches anywhere near to this perfection
of pattern, of pattern superficial and profound; but
the measure in which dramatists and poets approxi-
mate to this unity in a lifetime's work is one of the
measures of major poetry and drama. We feel a similar interest, in less degree, in the work of Jonson and
Chapman, and certainly in the unfinished work of
Marlowe; in less degree still, the interest is in the
work of Webster, baffling as the chronological order
of Webster's plays makes it. Even without an *œuvre,*
some dramatists can effect a satisfying unity and significance of pattern in single plays, a unity springing
from the depth and coherence of a number of emotions and feelings, and not only from dramatic and
poetic skill. The *Maid's Tragedy,* or *A King and No
King,* is better constructed, and has as many poetic
lines, as *The Changeling,* but is far inferior in the
degree of inner necessity in the feeling: something
more profound and more complex than what is
ordinarily called "sincerity."

It is significant that the first of Ford's important
plays to be performed, so far as we have knowledge,

is one which depends very patently upon some of the devices, and still more upon the feeling tone, of Shakespeare's last period. *The Lover's Melancholy* was licensed for the stage in 1628; it could hardly have been written but for *Cymbeline, The Winter's Tale, Pericles,* and *The Tempest.* Except for the comic passages, which are, as in all of Ford's plays, quite atrocious, it is a pleasant, dreamlike play without violence or exaggeration. As in other of his plays, there are verbal echoes of Shakespeare numerous enough; but what is more interesting is the use of the Recognition Scene, so important in Shakespeare's later plays, to the significance of which as a Shakespeare symbol Mr. Wilson Knight has drawn attention. In Shakespeare's plays, this is primarily the recognition of a long-lost daughter, secondarily of a wife; and we can hardly read the later plays attentively without admitting that the father and daughter theme was one of very deep symbolic value to him in his last productive years: Perdita, Marina, and Miranda share some beauty of which his earlier heroines do not possess the secret. Now Ford is struck by the dramatic and poetic effectiveness of the situation, and uses it on a level hardly higher than that of the device of twins in comedy; so in *The Lover's Melancholy* he introduces two such scenes, one the recognition of Eroclea in the guise of Parthenophil by her lover Palador, the second her recognition (accompanied, as in *Pericles,* by soft music) by her aged father Meleander. Both of these scenes are very well carried out, and in the first we have a passage in that slow solemn rhythm which is Ford's distinct contribution to the blank verse of the period.

> *Minutes are numbered by the fall of sands,*
> *As by an hourglass; the span of time*
> *Doth waste us to our graves, and we look on it:*
> *An age of pleasure, revelled out, comes home*
> *At last, and ends in sorrow; but the life,*
> *Weary of riot, numbers every sand,*
> *Wailing in sighs, until the last drop down;*
> *So to conclude calamity in rest.*

The tone and movement are so positive that when in a dull masque by Ford and Dekker, called *The Sun's Darling,* we come across such a passage as

> *Winter at last draws on the Night of Age;*
> *Yet still a humour of some novel fancy*
> *Untasted or untried, puts off the minute*
> *Of resolution, which should bid farewell*
> *To a vain world of weariness and sorrows. . . .*

we can hardly doubt the identity of the author. The scenes, as said above, are well planned and well written, and are even moving; but it is in such scenes as these that we are convinced of the incommensurability of writers like Ford (and Beaumont and Fletcher) with Shakespeare. It is not merely that they fail where he succeeds; it is that they had no conception of what he was trying to do; they speak another and cruder language. In their poetry there is no symbolic value; theirs is good poetry and good drama, but it is poetry and drama of the surface. And in a play like *The Revenger's Tragedy,* or *Women Beware Women,* or *The White Devil,* there is some of that inner significance which becomes the stronger and stronger undertone of Shakespeare's plays to the end. You do not find that in Ford.

It is suggested, then, that a dramatic poet cannot create characters of the greatest intensity of life unless his personages, in their reciprocal actions and behaviour in their story, are somehow dramatizing, but in no obvious form, an action or struggle for harmony in the soul of the poet. In this sense Ford's most famous, though not necessarily best, play may be called "meaningless"; and in so far as we may be justified in disliking its horrors, we are justified by its lack of meaning. *'Tis Pity She's a Whore* is surely one of the most read of minor Jacobean plays, and the only one of Ford's which has been lately revived upon the stage. It is the best constructed, with the exception of *Perkin Warbeck,* and the latter play is somewhat lacking in action. To the use of incest between brother and sister for a tragic plot there should be no objection of principle: the test is, however, whether the dramatic poet is able to give universal significance to a perversion of nature which, unlike some other aberrations, is defended by no one. The fact that it is defended by no one might, indeed, lend some colour of inoffensiveness to its dramatic use. Certainly, it is to Ford's credit that, having chosen this subject—which was suggested by an Italian tale—he went in for it thoroughly. There is none of the prurient flirting with impropriety which makes Beaumont and Fletcher's *King and No King* meretricious, and which is most evident and nauseous in the worst play which Ford himself ever wrote, *The Fancies Chaste and Noble;* a king of prurience from which the comedy of Wycherley is entirely free. Furthermore, Ford handles the theme with all the seriousness of which he is capable, and he can hardly be accused here of wanton sensationalism. It is not the sort of play which an age wholly corrupt would produce; and the signs of decay in Ford's age are more clearly visible in the plays of Beaumont and Fletcher than in his own. Ford does not make the unpleasant appear pleasant; and when, at the moment of avowed love, he makes Annabella say

Brother, even by our mother's dust, I charge you,
Do not betray me to your mirth or hate . . .

he is certainly double-stressing the horror, which from that moment he will never allow you to forget; but if he did not stress the horror he would be the more culpable. There is nothing in the play to which could be applied the term appropriately used in the advertisements of some films: the "peppy situation."

We must admit, too, that the versification and poetry, for example the fine speech of Annabella in Act v, sc. v, are of a very high order:

Brother, dear brother, know what I have been,
And know that now there's but a dining-time
'Twixt us and our confusion. . . .
Be not deceived, my brother;

> *This banquet is an harbinger of death*
> *To you and me; resolve yourself it is,*
> *And be prepared to welcome it.*

Finally, the low comedy, bad as it is, is more restrained in space, and more relevant to the plot, than
is usual with Ford; and the death of Bergetto ("Is
all this mine own blood?") is almost pathetic. When
all is said, however, there are serious shortcomings
to render account of. The sub-plot of Hippolita is
tedious, and her death superfluous. More important,
the passion of Giovanni and Annabella is not shown
as an affinity of temperament due to identity of
blood; it hardly rises above the purely carnal in-
fatuation. In *Antony and Cleopatra* (which is no
more an apology for adultery than *'Tis Pity* is an
apology for incest) we are made to feel convinced
of an overpowering attraction towards each other of
two persons, not only in defiance of conventional
morality, but against self-interest: an attraction as
fatal as that indicated by the love-potion motif in
Tristran und Isolde. We see clearly why Antony and
Cleopatra find each other congenial, and we see their
relation, during the course of the play, become
increasingly serious. But Giovanni is merely selfish
and self-willed, of a temperament to want a thing
the more because it is forbidden; Annabella is
pliant, vacillating and negative: the one almost a
monster of egotism, the other virtually a moral
defective. Her rebellious taunting of her violent
husband has an effect of naturalness and arouses
some sympathy; but the fact that Soranzo is himself

a bad lot does not extenuate her willingness to ruin him. In short, the play has not the general significance and emotional depth (for the two go together) without which no such action can be justified; and this defect separates it completely from the best plays of Webster, Middleton, and Tourneur.

There are two other plays, however, which are superior to *'Tis Pity She's a Whore.* The first is *The Broken Heart,* in which, with *'Tis Pity* and *The Lover's Melancholy,* we find some of the best "poetical" passages. Some of the best lines in *The Broken Heart* are given to the distraught Penthea; and being reminded of another fine passage given to a crazed woman in *Venice Preserved,* we might be tempted to generalize, and suggest that it is easier for an inferior dramatic poet to write poetry when he has a lunatic character to speak it, because in such passages he is less tied down to relevance and ordinary sense. The quite irrelevant and apparently meaningless lines

> *Remember,*
> *When we last gathered roses in the garden,*
> *I found my wits; but truly you lost yours.*

are perhaps the purest poetry to be found in the whole of Ford's writings; but the longer and better-known passage preceding them is also on a very high level:

> *Sure, if we were all Sirens, we should sing pitifully,*
> *And 'twere a comely music, when in parts*
> *One sung another's knell: the turtle sighs*

When he hath lost his mate; and yet some say
He must be dead first: 'tis a fine deceit
To pass away in a dream; indeed, I've slept
With mine eyes open a great while. No falsehood
Equals a broken faith; there's not a hair
Sticks on my head but, like a leaden plummet,
It sinks me to the grave: I must creep thither;
The journey is not long.

Between the first and the second of these passages
there is, however, a difference of kind rather than
degree: the first is real poetry, the second is the echo
of a mood which other dramatic poets had caught
and realized with greater mastery. Yet it exhibits
that which gives Ford his most certain claim to
perpetuity: the distinct personal rhythm in blank
verse which could be no one's but his alone.

As for the play itself, the plot is somewhat over-
loaded and distracted by the affairs of unfortunate
personages, all of whom have an equal claim on our
attention; Ford overstrains our pity and terror by
calling upon us to sympathize now with Penthea,
now with Calantha, now with Orgilus, now with
Ithocles; and the recipe by which good and evil are
mixed in the characters of Orgilus and Ithocles is
one which renders them less sympathetic, rather than
more human. The scene in which Calantha, during
the revels, is told successively the news of the death
of her father, of Penthea and of her betrothed, and
the scene in the temple which follows, must have
been very effective on the stage; and the style is
elevated and well sustained. The end of the play

almost deserves the extravagant commendation of Charles Lamb; but to a later critic it appears rather as a recrudescence of the Senecan mood:

They are the silent griefs which cut the heart-strings,
Let me die smiling.

than as a profound searching of the human heart. The best of the play, and it is Ford at his best, is the character and the action of Penthea, the lady who, after having been betrothed to the man she loves, is taken from him and given to a rival to gratify the ambitions of her brother. Even here, Ford misses an opportunity, and lapses in taste, by making the unloved husband, Bassanes, the vulgar jealous elderly husband of comedy: Penthea is a character which deserved, and indeed required, a more dignified and interesting foil. We are also diverted from her woes by the selfish revengefulness of her lost lover, who, having been robbed of happiness himself, is determined to contrive that no one else shall be happy. Penthea, on the other hand, commands all our sympathy when she pleads the cause of her brother Ithocles, the brother who has ruined her life, with the Princess Calantha whom he loves. She is throughout a dignified, consistent, and admirable figure; Penthea, and the Lady Katherine Gordon in *Perkin Warbeck,* are the most memorable of all Ford's characters.

Perkin Warbeck is little read, and does not contain any lines and passages such as those which remain in the memory after reading the other plays; but it is unquestionably Ford's highest achievement, and is one of the very best historical plays outside of the works of Shakespeare in the whole of Elizabethan and Jacobean drama. To make this base-born pretender to the throne of England into a dignified and heroic figure was no light task, and is not one which we should, after reading the other plays, have thought Ford competent to perform; but here for once there is no lapse of taste or judgment. Warbeck is made to appear as quite convinced that he is the lawful heir to the throne of England. We ourselves are left almost believing that he was; in the right state of uncertainty, wondering whether his kingly and steadfast behaviour is due to his royal blood, or merely due to his passionate conviction that he is of royal blood. What is more remarkable still, is that Ford has succeeded, not merely, as with Penthea, in creating one real person among shadows, but in fixing the right fitness and the right contrast between characters. Even at the end, when the earlier pretender, Lambert Simnel, who contentedly serves the King (Henry VII) in the humble capacity of falconer, is brought forward to plead with Perkin to accept a similar destiny, the scene is not degrading, but simply serves to emphasize the nobility and constancy of the hero. But to make a man who went down to history as an impostor into a heroic figure was not Ford's only difficulty and success. The King of Scotland, in order to demonstrate his faith, and emphasize his support, of Perkin Warbeck's claim to the English throne, gives him to wife his own niece, the Lady Katherine Gordon, very much against her father's wishes. To make a lady so abruptly given away to a stranger and dedicated to such very doubtful fortunes into not only a loyal but a devoted wife, is not easy; but Ford succeeds. The introduction of her admirer, her countryman Lord Dalyell, does not disturb the effect, for Katherine is not shown as having already reciprocated his affection. Dalyell is merely present as a reminder of the kind of happy and suitable marriage which Katherine would have made in her own country but for the appearance of Warbeck and the caprice of the King; and his touching devotion to her cause throughout the action only exhibits more beautifully her own devotion to her husband. Ford for once succeeded in a most difficult attempt; and the play of *Perkin Warbeck* is almost flawless.

Of Ford's other plays, *Love's Sacrifice* is reprinted in the Mermaid selection. It has a few fine scenes, but is disfigured by all the faults of which Ford was capable. In the complete editions—the Moxon edition with introduction (to Ford and Massinger) by Hartley Coleridge is obtainable, and there is also the edition of the Quarto texts published at the University of Louvain, the first volume edited by the late Professor Bang, and the second (1927) by Professor De Vocht—there are no other plays solely by Ford which retain any interest. It is difficult now to assent to Lamb's words, "Ford was of the first order of poets," or to Mr. Havelock Ellis's attempt (in his excellent introduction to the Mermaid volume) to present Ford as a modern man and a psychologist. Mr. Ellis makes the assertion that Ford is nearer to Stendhal and Flaubert than he is to Shakespeare. Ford, nevertheless, depended upon

Shakespeare; but it would be truer to say that Shakespeare is nearer to Stendhal and Flaubert than he is to Ford. There is a very important distinction to be drawn at this point. Stendhal and Flaubert, and to them might be added Balzac, are analysts of the individual soul as it is found in a particular phase of society; and in their work is found as much sociology as individual psychology. Indeed, the two are aspects of one thing; and the greater French novelists, from Stendhal to Proust, chronicle the rise, the régime, and the decay of the upper bourgeoisie in France. In Elizabethan and Jacobean drama, and even in the comedy of Congreve and Wycherley, there is almost no analysis of the particular society of the times, except in so far as it records the rise of the City families, and their ambition to ally themselves with needy peerages and to acquire country estates. Even that rise of the City, in *Eastward Hoe* and *Michaelmas Terme,* is treated lightly as a foible of the age, and not as a symptom of social decay and change. It is indeed in the lack of this sense of a "changing world," of corruptions and abuses peculiar to their own time, that the Elizabethan and Jacobean dramatists are blessed. We feel that they believed in their own age, in a way in which no nineteenth- or twentieth-century writer of the greatest seriousness has been able to believe in his age. And accepting their age, they were in a position to concentrate their attention, to their respective abilities, upon the common characteristics of humanity in all ages, rather than upon the differences. We can partly criticize their age through our study of them, but they did not so criticize it themselves. In the work of Shakespeare as a whole, there is to be read the profoundest and indeed one of the most sombre studies of humanity that has ever been made in poetry; though it is in fact so comprehensive that we cannot qualify it as a whole as either glad or sorry. We recognize the same assumption of permanence in his minor fellows. Dante held it also, and the great Greek dramatists. In periods of unsettlement and change we do not observe this: it was a changing world which met the eyes of Lucian or of Petronius. But in the kind of analysis in which Shakespeare was supreme the other Elizabethans and Jacobean dramatists differed only in degree and in comprehensiveness.

Such observations are not made in order to cast doubt upon the ultimate value or the permanence of the greatest nineteenth-century fiction. But for the age in which Shakespeare lived and the age into which his influence extended after his death, it must be his work, and his work as a whole, that is our criterion. The whole of Shakespeare's work is *one* poem; and it is the poetry of it in this sense, not the poetry of isolated lines and passages or the poetry of the single figures which he created, that matters most. A man might, hypothetically, compose any number of fine passages or even of whole poems which would each give satisfaction, and yet not be a great poet, unless we felt them to be united by one significant, consistent, and developing personality. Shakespeare is the one, among all his contemporaries, who fulfils these conditions; and the nearest to him is Marlowe. Jonson and Chapman have the consistency, but a far lower degree of significant development; Middleton and Webster take a lower place than these; the author of *The Revenger's Tragedy*, whether we call him Tourneur or Middleton or another, accomplishes all that can be accomplished within the limits of a single play. But in all these dramatists there is the essential, as well as the superficies, of poetry; they give the pattern, or we may say the undertone, of the personal emotion, the personal drama and struggle, which no biography, however full and intimate, could give us; which nothing can give us but our experience of the plays themselves. Ford, as well as Fletcher, wrote enough plays for us to see the absence of essential poetry. Ford's poetry, as well as Beaumont and Fletcher's, is of the surface: that is to say, it is the result of the stock of expressions of feeling accumulated by the greater men. It is the absence of purpose—if we may use the word "purpose" for something more profound than any formulable purpose can be—in such dramatists as Ford, Beaumont, Fletcher, Shirley, and later Otway, and still later Shelley, which makes their drama tend towards mere sensationalism. Many reasons might be found, according to the particular historical aspects from which we consider the problem. But Ford, as dramatic poet, as writer of dramatic blank verse, has one quality which assures him of a higher place than even Beaumont and Fletcher; and that is a quality which any poet may

envy him. The varieties of cadence and tone in blank
verse are none too many, in the history of English
verse; and Ford, though intermittently, was able
to manipulate sequences of words in blank verse
in a manner which is quite his own.

Philip Massinger

Massinger has been more fortunately and more fairly judged than several of his greater contemporaries. Three critics have done their best by him: the notes of Coleridge exemplify Coleridge's fragmentary and fine perceptions; the essay of Leslie Stephen is a piece of formidable destructive analysis; and the essay of Swinburne is Swinburne's criticism at its best. None of these, probably, has put Massinger finally and irrefutably into a place.

English criticism is inclined to argue or persuade rather than to state; and, instead of forcing the subject to expose himself, these critics have left in their work an undissolved residuum of their own good taste, which, however impeccable, is something that requires our faith. The principles which animate this taste remain unexplained. Canon Cruickshank's book[1] is a work of scholarship; and the advantage of good scholarship is that it presents us with evidence which is an invitation to the critical faculty

[1] *Philip Massinger,* by A. H. Cruickshank (Oxford: Blackwell, 1920).

of the reader: it bestows a method, rather than a judgment.

It is difficult—it is perhaps the supreme difficulty of criticism—to make the facts generalize themselves; but Mr. Cruickshank at least presents us with facts which are capable of generalization. This is a service of value; and it is therefore wholly a compliment to the author to say that his appendices are as valuable as the essay itself.

The sort of labour to which Mr. Cruickshank has devoted himself is one that professed critics ought more willingly to undertake. It is an important part of criticism, more important than any mere expression of opinion. To understand Elizabethan drama it is necessary to study a dozen playwrights at once, to dissect with all care the complex growth, to ponder collaboration to the utmost line. Reading Shakespeare and several of his contemporaries is pleasure enough, perhaps all the pleasure possible, for most. But if we wish to consummate and refine this pleasure by understanding it, to distil the last drop of it, to press and press the essence of each author, to apply exact measurement to our own sensations, then we must compare; and we cannot compare without parcelling the threads of authorship and influence. We must employ Mr. Cruickshank's judgments; and perhaps the most important judgment to which he has committed himself is this:

"Massinger, in his grasp of stagecraft, his flexible metre, his desire in the sphere of ethics to exploit both vice and virtue, is typical of an age which had much culture, but which, without being exactly corrupt, lacked moral fibre."

Here, in fact, is our text: to elucidate this sentence would be to account for Massinger. We begin vaguely with good taste, by a recognition that Massinger is inferior: can we trace this inferiority, dissolve it, and have left any element of merit?

We turn first to the parallel quotations from Massinger and Shakespeare collocated by Mr. Cruickshank to make manifest Massinger's indebtedness. One of the surest of tests is the way in which a poet borrows. Immature poets imitate; mature poets steal; bad poets deface what they take, and good poets make it into something better, or at least something different. The good poet welds his theft into a whole of feeling which is unique, utterly different from that from which it was torn; the bad poet throws it into something which has no cohesion. A good poet will usually borrow from authors remote in time, or alien in language, or diverse in interest. Chapman borrowed from Seneca; Shakespeare and Webster from Montaigne. The two great followers of Shakespeare, Webster and Tourneur, in their mature work do not borrow from him; he is too close to them to be of use to them in this way. Massinger, as Mr. Cruickshank shows, borrows from Shakespeare a good deal. Let us profit by some of the quotations with which he has provided us—

MASSINGER:

> *Can I call back yesterday, with all their rids*
> *That bow unto my sceptre? or restore*

> *My mind to that tranquillity and peace*
> *It then enjoyed?*

SHAKESPEARE:

> *Not poppy, nor mandragora,*
> *Nor all the drowsy syrops of the world*
> *Shall ever medicine thee to that sweet sleep*
> *Which thou owedst yesterday.*

Massinger's is a general rhetorical question, the language just and pure, but colourless. Shakespeare's has particular significance; and the adjective "drowsy" and the verb "medicine" infuse a precise vigour. This is, on Massinger's part, an echo, rather than an imitation or a plagiarism—the basest, because least conscious, form of borrowing. "Drowsy syrop" is a condensation of meaning frequent in Shakespeare, but rare in Massinger.

MASSINGER:

> *Thou didst not borrow of Vice her indirect,*
> *Crooked, and abject means.*

SHAKESPEARE:

> *God knows, my son;*
> *By what by-paths and indirect crook'd ways*
> *I met this crown.*

Here, again, Massinger gives the general forensic statement, Shakespeare the particular image. "Indirect crook'd" is forceful in Shakespeare; a mere pleonasm in Massinger. "Crook'd ways" is a metaphor; Massinger's phrase only the ghost of a metaphor.

MASSINGER:

> And now, in the evening,
> When thou should'st pass with honour to thy
> rest,
> Wilt thou fall like a meteor?

SHAKESPEARE:

> I shall fall
> Like a bright exhalation in the evening,
> And no man see me more.

Here the lines of Massinger have their own beauty. Still, a "bright exhalation" appears to the eye and makes us catch our breath in the evening; "meteor" is a dim simile; the word is worn.

MASSINGER:

> What you deliver to me shall be lock'd up
> In a strong cabinet, of which you yourself
> Shall keep the key.

SHAKESPEARE:

> 'Tis in my memory locked,
> And you yourself shall keep the key of it.

In the preceding passage Massinger had squeezed his simile to death, here he drags it round the city at his heels; and how swift Shakespeare's figure is! We may add two more passages, not given by our commentator; here the model is Webster. They occur on the same page, an artless confession.

> *Here he comes,*
> *His nose held up; he hath something in the wind,*

is hardly comparable to

The Cardinal lifts up his nose like a foul porpoise
*   before a storm,*

and when we come upon

*   as tann'd galley-slaves*
Pay such as do redeem them from the oar

it is unnecessary to turn up the great lines in the *Duchess of Malfy.* Massinger fancied this galley-slave; for he comes with his oar again in *The Bondman*—

Never did galley-slave shake off his chains,
Or looked on his redemption from the oar. . . .

Now these are mature plays; and *The Roman Actor* (from which we have drawn the two previous extracts) is said to have been the preferred play of its author.

We may conclude directly from these quotations that Massinger's feeling for language had outstripped his feeling for things; that his eye and his vocabulary were not in co-operation. One of the greatest distinctions of several of his elder contemporaries—we name Middleton, Webster, Tourneur—is a gift for combining, for fusing into a single phrase, two or more diverse impressions.

. . . in her strong toil of grace

of Shakespeare is such a fusion; the metaphor identifies itself with what suggests it; the resultant is one and is unique—

Does the silk worm expend *her* yellow labours? . . .
Why does yon fellow falsify highways
And lays his life between the judge's lips
To refine *such a one? keeps horse and men*
To beat their valours *for her?*

Let the common sewer take it from distinction. . . .
Lust and forgetfulness have been amongst us. . . .

These lines of Tourneur and of Middleton exhibit
that perpetual slight alteration of language, words
perpetually juxtaposed in new and sudden combi-
nations, meanings perpetually *eingeschachtelt* into
meanings, which evidences a very high development
of the senses, a development of the English language
which we have perhaps never equalled. And, indeed,
with the end of Chapman, Middleton, Webster,
Tourneur, Donne we end a period when the intellect
was immediately at the tips of the senses. Sensation
became word and word was sensation. The next
period is the period of Milton (though still with
a Marvell in it); and this period is initiated by
Massinger.

It is not that the word becomes less exact. Massinger is, in a wholly eulogistic sense, choice and
correct. And the decay of the senses is not inconsistent with a greater sophistication of language. But
every vital development in language is a development of feeling as well. The verse of Shakespeare
and the major Shakespearean dramatists is an innovation of this kind, a true mutation of species.
The verse practised by Massinger is a different verse
from that of his predecessors; but it is not a develop-

ment based on, or resulting from, a new way of feeling. On the contrary, it seems to lead us away from feeling altogether.

We mean that Massinger must be placed as much at the beginning of one period as at the end of another. A certain Boyle, quoted by Mr. Cruickshank, says that Milton's blank verse owes much to the study of Massinger's.

"In the indefinable touches which make up the music of a verse [says Boyle], in the artistic distribution of pauses, and in the unerring choice and grouping of just those words which strike the ear as the perfection of harmony, there are, if we leave Cyril Tourneur's *Atheist's Tragedy* out of the question, only two masters in the drama, Shakespeare in his latest period and Massinger."

This Boyle must have had a singular ear to have preferred Tourneur's secondary work to his *Revenger's Tragedy,* and one must think that he had never glanced at Ford. But though the appraisal be ludicrous, the praise is not undeserved. Mr. Cruickshank has given us an excellent example of Massinger's syntax—

> *What though my father*
> *Writ man before he was so, and confirm'd it,*
> *By numbering that day no part of his life*
> *In which he did not service to his country;*
> *Was he to be free therefore from the laws*
> *And ceremonious form in your decrees?*
> *Or else because he did as much as man*
> *In those three memorable overthrows,*

> *At Granson, Morat, Nancy, where his master,*
> *The warlike Charalois, with whose misfortunes*
> *I bear his name, lost treasure, men, and life,*
> *To be excused from payment of those sums*
> *Which (his own patrimony spent) his zeal*
> *To serve his country forced him to take up!*

It is impossible to deny the masterly construction of this passage; perhaps there is not one living poet who could do the like. It is impossible to deny the originality. The language is pure and correct, free from muddiness or turbidity. Massinger does not confuse metaphors, or heap them one upon another. He is lucid, though not easy. But if Massinger's age, "without being exactly corrupt, lacks moral fibre," Massinger's verse, without being exactly corrupt, suffers from cerebral anaemia. To say that an involved style is necessarily a bad style would be preposterous. But such a style should follow the involutions of a mode of perceiving, registering, and digesting impressions which is also involved. It is to be feared that the feeling of Massinger is simple and overlaid with received ideas. Had Massinger had a nervous system as refined as that of Middleton, Tourneur, Webster, or Ford, his style would be a triumph. But such a nature was not at hand, and Massinger precedes, not another Shakespeare, but Milton.

Massinger is, in fact, at a further remove from Shakespeare than that other precursor of Milton—John Fletcher. Fletcher was above all an opportunist, in his verse, in his momentary effects, never quite a

pastiche; in his structure ready to sacrifice everything to the single scene. To Fletcher, because he
was more intelligent, less will be forgiven. Fletcher
had a cunning guess at feelings, and betrayed them;
Massinger was unconscious and innocent. As an
artisan of the theatre he is not inferior to Fletcher,
and his best tragedies have an honester unity than
Bonduca. But the unity is superficial. In *The Roman
Actor* the development of parts is out of all proportion to the central theme; in *The Unnatural Combat,*
in spite of the deft handling of suspense and the
quick shift from climax to a new suspense, the
first part of the play is the hatred of Malefort for
his son and the second part is his passion for his
daughter. It is theatrical skill, not an artistic
conscience arranging emotions, that holds the two
parts together. In *The Duke of Milan* the appearance
of Sforza at the Court of his conqueror only delays
the action, or rather breaks the emotional rhythm.
And we have named three of Massinger's best.

A dramatist who so skilfully welds together parts
which have no reason for being together, who
fabricates plays so well knit and so remote from
unity, we should expect to exhibit the same synthetic
cunning in character. Mr. Cruickshank, Coleridge,
and Leslie Stephen are pretty well agreed that Massinger is no master of characterization. You can, in
fact, put together heterogeneous parts to form a lively
play; but a character, to be living, must be conceived from some emotional unity. A character is
not to be composed of scattered observations of
human nature, but of parts which are felt together.

Hence it is that although Massinger's failure to
draw a moving character is no greater than his failure
to make a whole play, and probably springs from
the same defective sensitiveness, yet the failure in
character is more conspicuous and more disastrous.
A "living" character is not necessarily "true to life."
It is a person whom we can see and hear, whether
he be true or false to human nature as we know it.
What the creator of character needs is not so much
knowledge of motives as keen sensibility; the dramatist need not understand people; but he must be
exceptionally aware of them. This awareness was
not given to Massinger. He inherits the traditions
of conduct, female chastity, hymeneal sanctity, the
fashion of honour, without either criticizing or
informing them from his own experience. In the
earlier drama these conventions are merely a framework, or an alloy necessary for working the metal;
the metal itself consisted of unique emotions resulting inevitably from the circumstances, resulting
or inhering as inevitably as the properties of a
chemical compound. Middleton's heroine, for instance, in *The Changeling,* exclaims in the well-
known words—

Why, 'tis impossible thou canst be so wicked,
To shelter such a cunning cruelty
To make his death the murderer of my honour!

The word "honour" in such a situation is out of
date, but the emotion of Beatrice at that moment,
given the conditions, is as permanent and substantial
as anything in human nature. The emotion of

Othello in Act v is the emotion of a man who discovers that the worst part of his own soul has been
exploited by some one more clever than he; it is
this emotion carried by the writer to a very high
degree of intensity. Even in so late and so decayed
a drama as that of Ford, the framework of emotions
and morals of the time is only the vehicle for
statements of feeling which are unique and im-
perishable: Ford's and Ford's only.

What may be considered corrupt or decadent in
the morals of Massinger is not an alteration or
diminution in morals; it is simply the disappearance
of all the personal and real emotions which this
morality supported and into which it introduced a
kind of order. As soon as the emotions disappear
the morality which ordered it appears hideous.
Puritanism itself became repulsive only when it
appeared as the survival of a restraint after the
feelings which it restrained had gone. When Massinger's ladies resist temptation they do not appear
to undergo any important emotion; they merely
know what is expected of them; they manifest themselves to us as lubricous prudes. Any age has its
conventions; and any age might appear absurd
when its conventions get into the hands of a man
like Massinger—a man, we mean, of so exceptionally
superior a literary talent as Massinger's, and so
paltry an imagination. The Elizabethan morality was
an important convention; important because it was
not consciously of one social class alone, because it
provided a framework for emotions to which all
classes could respond, and it hindered no feeling. It

was not hypocritical, and it did not suppress; its dark corners are haunted by the ghost of Mary Fitton and perhaps greater. It is a subject which has not been sufficiently investigated. Fletcher and Massinger rendered it ridiculous; not by not believing it, but because they were men of great talents who could not vivify it; because they could not fit into it passionate, complete human characters.

The tragedy of Massinger is interesting chiefly according to the definition given before; the highest degree of verbal excellence compatible with the most rudimentary development of the senses. Massinger succeeds better in something which is not tragedy; in the romantic comedy. *A Very Woman* deserves all the praise that Swinburne, with his almost unerring gift of selection, has bestowed upon it. The probable collaboration of Fletcher had the happiest results; for certainly that admirable comic personage, the tipsy Borachia, is handled with more humour than we expect of Massinger. It is a play which would be enjoyable on the stage. The form, however, of romantic comedy is itself inferior and decadent. There is an inflexibility about the poetic drama which is by no means a matter of classical, or neo-classical, or pseudo-classical law. The poetic drama might develop forms highly different from those of Greece or England, India or Japan. Conceded the utmost freedom, the romantic drama would yet remain inferior. The poetic drama must have an emotional unity, let the emotion be whatever you like. It must have a dominant tone; and if this be strong enough, the most heterogeneous emotions

may be made to reinforce it. The romantic comedy
is a skilful concoction of inconsistent emotion, a
revue of emotion. *A Very Woman* is surpassingly
well plotted. The debility of romantic drama does
not depend upon extravagant setting, or preposterous
events, or inconceivable coincidences; all these might
be found in a serious tragedy or comedy. It consists
in an internal incoherence of feelings, a concatena-
tion of emotions which signifies nothing.

From this type of play, so eloquent of emotional
disorder, there was no swing back of the pendulum.
Changes never come by a simple reinfusion into the
form which the life has just left. The romantic drama
was not a new form. Massinger dealt not with emotions so much as with the social abstractions of emotions, more generalized and therefore more quickly
and easily interchangeable within the confines of a
single action. He was not guided by direct com-
munications through the nerves. Romantic drama
tended, accordingly, towards what is sometimes called
the "typical," but which is not the truly typical; for
the *typical* figure in a drama is always particularized
—an individual. The tendency of the romantic drama
was towards a form which continued it in removing
its more conspicuous vices, was towards a more severe
external order. This form was the Heroic Drama.
We look into Dryden's "Essay on Heroic Plays," and
we find that "love and valour ought to be the subject of an heroic poem." Massinger, in his destruction
of the old drama, had prepared the way for Dryden.
The intellect had perhaps exhausted the old con-

ventions. It was not able to supply the impoverish-
ment of feeling.

Such are the reflections aroused by an examination
of some of Massinger's plays in the light of Mr.
Cruickshank's statement that Massinger's age "had
much more culture, but, without being exactly corrupt, lacked moral fibre." The statement may be
supported. In order to fit into our estimate of Massinger the two admirable comedies—*A New Way to
Pay Old Debts* and *The City Madam*—a more extensive research would be required than is possible
within our limits.

II

Massinger's tragedy may be summarized for the un-
prepared reader as being very dreary. It is dreary,
unless one is prepared by a somewhat extensive
knowledge of his livelier contemporaries to grasp
without fatigue precisely the elements in it which
are capable of giving pleasure; or unless one is in-
cited by a curious interest in versification. In comedy,
however, Massinger was one of the few masters in the
language. He was a master in a comedy which is
serious, even sombre; and in one aspect of it there
are only two names to mention with his: Those of
Marlowe and Jonson. In comedy, as a matter of fact,
a greater variety of methods were discovered and
employed than in tragedy. The method of Kyd, as
developed by Shakespeare, was the standard for
English tragedy down to Otway and to Shelley. But

both individual temperament, and varying epochs,
made more play with comedy. The comedy of Lyly
is one thing; that of Shakespeare, followed by Beaumont and Fletcher, is another; and that of Middleton is a third. And Massinger, while he has his own
comedy, is nearer to Marlowe and Jonson than to
any of these.

Massinger was, in fact, as a comic writer, fortunate
in the moment at which he wrote. His comedy is
transitional; but it happens to be one of those transitions which contain some merit not anticipated by
predecessors or refined upon by later writers. The
comedy of Jonson is nearer to caricature; that of
Middleton a more photographic delineation of low
life. Massinger is nearer to Restoration comedy, and
more like his contemporary, Shirley, in assuming a
certain social level, certain distinctions of class, as
a postulate of his comedy. This resemblance to later
comedy is also the important point of difference between Massinger and earlier comedy. But Massinger's
comedy differs just as widely from the comedy of
manners proper; he is closer to that in his romantic
drama—in *A Very Woman*—than in *A New Way to
Pay Old Debts;* in his comedy his interest is not in
the follies of love-making or the absurdities of social
pretence, but in the unmasking of villainy. Just as
the Old Comedy of Molière differs in principle from
the New Comedy of Marivaux, so the Old Comedy of
Massinger differs from the New Comedy of his contemporary Shirley. And as in France, so in England,
the more farcical comedy was the more serious. Mas-

singer's great comic rogues, Sir Giles Overreach and
Luke Frugal, are members of the large English
family which includes Barabas and Sir Epicure Mammon, and from which Sir Tunbelly Clumsy claims
descent.

What distinguishes Massinger from Marlowe and
Jonson is in the main an inferiority. The greatest
comic characters of these two dramatists are slight
work in comparison with Shakespeare's best—Falstaff has a third dimension and Epicure Mammon
has only two. But this slightness is part of the nature
of the art which Jonson practised, a smaller art than
Shakespeare's. The inferiority of Massinger to Jonson
is an inferiority, not of one type of art to another,
but within Jonson's type. It is a simple deficiency.
Marlowe's and Jonson's comedies were a view of life;
they were, as great literature is, the transformation
of a personality into a personal work of art, their
lifetime's work, long or short. Massinger is not simply
a smaller personality: his personality hardly exists.
He did not, out of his own personality, build a world
of art, as Shakespeare and Marlowe and Jonson
built.

In the fine pages which Remy de Gourmont devotes to Flaubert in his *Problème du Style,* the great
critic declares:

"La vie est un dépouillement. Le but de l'activité
propre de l'homme est de nettoyer sa personnalité,
de la laver de toutes les souillures qu'y déposa l'édu-
cation, de la dégager de toutes les empreintes qu'y
laissèrent nos admirations adolescentes";

and again:

"Flaubert incorporait toute sa sensibilité à ses
œuvres. . . . Hors de ses livres, où il se transvasait
goutte à gouette, jusqu'à la lie, Flaubert est fort peu
intéressant."

Of Shakespeare notably, of Jonson less, of Marlowe
(and of Keats to the term of life allowed him), one
can say that they *se transvasaient goutte à gouette;*
and in England, which has produced a prodigious
number of men of genius and comparatively few
works of art, there are not many writers of whom
one can say it. Certainly not of Massinger. A brilliant master of technique, he was not, in this profound sense, an artist. And so we come to inquire
how, if this is so, he could have written two great
comedies. We shall probably be obliged to conclude
that a large part of their excellence is, in some way
which should be defined, fortuitous; and that therefore they are, however remarkable, not works of perfect art.

This objection raised by Leslie Stephen to Massinger's method of revealing a villain has great cogency; but I am inclined to believe that the cogency
is due to a somewhat different reason from that
which Leslie Stephen assigns. His statement is too
apriorist to be quite trustworthy. There is no reason
why a comedy or a tragedy villain should not declare himself, and in as long a period as the author
likes; but the sort of villain who may run on in this
way is a simple villain (simple not *simpliste*). Barabas and Volpone can declare their character, be-

cause they have no inside; appearance and reality are coincident; they are forces in particular directions. Massinger's two villains are not simple. Giles Overreach is essentially a great force directed upon small objects; a great force; a small mind; the terror of a dozen parishes instead of the conqueror of a world. The force is misapplied, attenuated, thwarted, by the man's vulgarity: he is a great man of the City, without fear, but with the most abject awe of the aristocracy. He is accordingly not simple, but a product of a certain civilization, and he is not wholly conscious. His monologues are meant to be, not what he thinks he is, but what he really is: and yet they are not the truth about him, and he himself certainly does not know the truth. To declare himself, therefore, is impossible.

Nay, when my ears are pierced with widows' cries,
And undone orphans wash with tears my threshold,
I only think what 'tis to have my daughter
Right honourable; and 'tis a powerful charm
Makes me insensible of remorse, or pity,
Or the least sting of conscience.

This is the wrong note. Elsewhere we have the right:

                   Thou art a fool;
In being out of office, I am out of danger;
Where, if I were a justice, besides the trouble,
I might or out of wilfulness, or error,
Run myself finely into a praemunire,
And so become a prey to the informer,

No, I'll have none of 't; 'tis enough I keep
Greedy at my devotion: so he serve
My purposes, let him hang, or damn, I care not . . .

And how well tuned, well modulated, here, the
diction! The man is audible and visible. But from
passages like the first we may be permitted to infer
that Massinger was unconscious of trying to develop
a different kind of character from any that Marlowe
or Jonson had invented.

Luke Frugal, in *The City Madam*, is not so great
a character as Sir Giles Overreach. But Luke Frugal
just misses being almost the greatest of all hypo-
crites. His humility in the first act of the play is more
than half real. The error in his portraiture is not the
extravagant hocus-pocus of supposed Indian necro-
mancers by which he is so easily duped, but the pre-
mature disclosure of villainy in his temptation of the
two apprentices of his brother. But for this, he would
be a perfect chameleon of circumstance. Here, again,
we feel that Massinger was conscious only of in-
venting a rascal of the old simpler farce type. But the
play is not a farce, in the sense in which *The Jew of
Malta, The Alchemist, Bartholomew Fair* are farces.
Massinger had not the personality to create great
farce, and he was too serious to invent trivial farce.
The ability to perform that slight distortion of *all*
the elements in the world of a play or a story, so that
this world is complete in itself, which was given to
Marlowe and Jonson (and to Rabelais) and which is
prerequisite to great farce, was denied to Massinger.
On the other hand, his temperament was more closely

related to theirs than to that of Shirley or the Restoration wits. His two comedies therefore occupy a place by themselves. His ways of thinking and feeling isolate him from both the Elizabethan and the later Caroline mind. He might almost have been a great realist; he is killed by conventions which were suitable for the preceding literary generation, but not for his. Had Massinger been a greater man, a man of more intellectual courage, the current of English literature immediately after him might have taken a different course. The defect is precisely a defect of personality. He is not, however, the only man of letters who, at the moment when a new view of life is wanted, has looked at life through the eyes of his predecessors, and only at manners through his own.

John Marston

John Marston, the dramatist, has been dead for three hundred years. The date of his death, June 25th, 1634, is one of the few certain facts that we know about him; but the appearance of the first volume of a new edition of his works, as well as an edition of his best-known play by itself, is a more notable event than the arrival of his tercentenary.[1] For Marston has enjoyed less attention, from either scholars or critics, than any of his contemporaries of equal or greater rank; and for both scholars and critics he remains a territory of unexplored riches and risks. The position of most of his contemporaries is pretty well settled; one cannot go very far wrong in one's estimate of the dramatists with whom Marston worked; but about Marston a wide divergency of opinion is still possible. His greater defects are such as anyone can see; his merits are still a matter for controversy.

[1] *The Plays of John Marston,* in three volumes, edited by H. Harvey Wood, Volume I (Edinburgh: Oliver and Boyd, 8s. 6d. net each).

The Malcontent, edited by G. B. Harrison, The Temple Dramatists (Dent: 1s. 6d. net).

Little has transpired of the events of Marston's life since Bullen presented in 1887 what has hitherto been the standard edition. The date and place of his birth have been unsettled; but the main facts—that his mother was Italian, that he was educated at Brasenose College and put to the law, that he wrote satires and then plays for a brief period and finally entered the Church—are undisputed. We are left with the unsupported statement of Ben Jonson that he beat Marston and took away his pistol; but, without necessarily impugning the veracity of Jonson, or suggesting that he wished to impress Drummond with his own superiority, having gone such a long journey to talk to him, we may do well to put aside the image of a mean and ridiculous figure which Jonson has left us before considering the value of Marston's work. And before reading the selections of Lamb, or the encomium of Swinburne, we should do better to read the plays of Marston—there are not many—straight through. Did Marston have anything of his own to say or not? Was he really a dramatist, or only a playwright through force of circumstances? And if he was a dramatist, in which of his plays was he at his best? In answering these questions we have, as with no other Elizabethan dramatist, the opportunity to go completely wrong; and that opportunity is an incentive.

Dr. Wood's first volume includes, besides *Antonio and Mellida* and *Antonio's Revenge, The Malcontent.* There are three quartos of *The Malcontent:* Dr. Wood tells us that he has followed the second (B in Dr. Greg's classification), but has adopted what

seemed to him better and fuller readings from A and
C. Dr. Harrison's text is, he tells us, the "revised
quarto," and he follows the Temple Dramatists principle (certainly the right one for such a series) of
modernized spelling and punctuation. Our only com-
plaint against both editors is that they have con-
scientiously limited themselves, in their notes, to
what is verifiable, and have deprived themselves and
their readers of that delight in aside and conjecture
which the born annotator exploits. Dr. Harrison's
glossary, for instance, omits some difficult words,
but includes others of which the meaning is obvious;
one wishes that editors of Elizabethan texts would
take as their model that perfect annotator Mr. F. L.
Lucas in his monumental edition of John Webster.
Dr. Wood appears to have had the advantage of
consulting Dr. Harrison's edition; and it must be
said that they both refer the reader to Mr. Lucas's
edition of Webster for fuller information on certain
points. Both Dr. Wood and Dr. Harrison seem to
be assured on one critical judgment: that *The Malcontent* is the most important of Marston's plays.
Dr. Harrison says forthright: "*The Malcontent* is
Marston's best play." Dr. Wood says only:

"The best of Marston's comedies and tragedies,
and his great tragi-comedy, *The Malcontent,* have
striking and original qualities. . . . *The Malcontent*
is one of the most original plays of its period. . . ."

It is this assumption that we are privileged to examine.

If we read first the two plays with which collected
editions, including Dr. Wood's, begin—*Antonio and*

Mellida and *Antonio's Revenge*—our first impression is likely to be one of bewilderment, that anyone could write plays so bad and that plays so bad could be preserved and reprinted. Yet they are not plays that one wholly forgets; and the second reading, undertaken perhaps out of curiosity to know why such bad plays are remembered, may show that the problem is by no means simple. One at first suspects Marston to have been a poet, with no inclination to the stage, but driven thereto by need, and trying to write to the popular taste; just as a fastidious writer of to-day may produce, under financial pressure, something which he vainly imagines to be a potential best-seller. There is one immediate objection to this theory, even before we have read Marston's later work. It is that there is better *poetry* in these two plays, both in several passages, quotable and quoted, and in the general atmosphere, than there is in the *Satires, The Scourge of Villainy,* or *Pygmalion.* The last of these was apparently an attempt to repeat the success of *Venus and Adonis,* and deserves only the fate of every piece of writing which is an attempt to do again what has already been done by a better man. The first are obviously lacking in personal conviction. The Satire, when all is said and done, is a form which the Elizabethans endeavoured to naturalize with very slight success; it is not until Oldham that a satire appears, sufficiently natural to be something more than a literary exercise. When Donne tries it, he is not any more successful than Marston; but Donne could write in no form without showing that he was a poet, and though his satires are not good satires, there is enough poetry in them, as in his epistles, to make them worth reading. Marston is very competent, and perfectly perfunctory. He wrote satires, as he wrote *Pygmalion,* in order to succeed; and when he found that the satire was more likely to lead him to the gaol than to success, he seems to have taken up, in the same spirit, the writing of plays. And however laboured the first two tragical plays may be, there is more poetry in them than in anything he had written before. So we cannot say that he was a "poet," forced by necessity to become a "dramatist."

The second observation upon *Antonio and Mellida* and its sequel, if we may call "sequel" a play of such different intent, is that their badness cannot be explained simply by incapacity, or even by plain carelessness. A blockhead could not have written them; a painstaking blockhead would have done better; and a careless master, or a careless dunce, would not have gone out of his way to produce the effects of nonsensicality which we meet. These two plays give the effect of work done by a man who was so exasperated by having to write in a form which he despised that he deliberately wrote worse than he could have written, in order to relieve his feelings. This may appear an over-ingenious apologetic; but it is difficult to explain, by any natural action of mediocrity the absurd dialogue in Italian in which Antonio and Mellida suddenly express themselves in Act IV, Sc. i. The versification, such as it is, has for the most part no poetic merit; when it is most intelligible, as in the apostrophes of Andrugio, it is aiming at a conventional noble effect; but it has often, and more interestingly, a peculiar jerkiness and irritability, as of a writer who is, for some obscure reason, wrought to the pitch of exasperation. There are occasional reversions to an earlier vocabulary and movement, difficult to explain at the very end of the sixteenth century, reversions which to Ben Jonson must have seemed simple evidence of technical incompetence. As in the Prologue to *Antonio's Revenge:*

> *The rawish dank of clumsy winter ramps*
> *The fluent summer's vein; and drizzling sleet*
> *Chilleth the wan bleak cheek of the numb'd earth,*
> *While snarling gusts nibble the juiceless leaves*
> *From the nak'd shuddering branch. . . .*

or the line at the beginning of Act II:

> *The black jades of swart night trot foggy rings*
> *'Bout heaven's brow. . . .*

It is not only in passages such as these that we get the impression of having to do with a personality which is at least unusual and difficult to catalogue. Marston's minor comic characters, in these two plays, are as completely lifeless as the major characters. Whether decent or indecent, their drollery is as far from mirth-provoking as can be: a continuous and tedious rattle of dried peas. And yet something is conveyed, after a time, by the very emptiness and irrelevance of this empty and irrelevant gabble; there is a kind of significant lifelessness in this shadow-show. There is no more unarticulated scarecrow in the whole of Elizabethan drama than Sir Jeffrey Balurdo. Yet Act v, Sc. i of *Antonio's Revenge* leaves some impression upon the mind, though what it is we may not be able to say.

"Ho, who's above there, ho? A murrain on all proverbs. They say hunger breaks through stone walls; but I am as gaunt as lean-ribbed famine, yet I can burst through no stone walls. O now, Sir Jeffrey, show thy valour, break prison and be hanged. Nor shall the darkest nook of hell contain the discontented Sir Balurdo's ghost. Well, I am out well; I have put off the prison to put on the rope. O poor shotten herring, what a pickle art thou in! O hunger, how thou domineer'st in my guts! O for a fat leg of ewe mutton in stewed broth, or drunken song to feed on! I could belch rarely, for I am all wind. O cold, cold, cold, cold, cold. O poor knight! O poor Sir Jeffrey, sing like an unicorn before thou dost dip thy horn in the water of death. O cold, O sing, O cold, O poor Sir Jeffrey, sing, sing!"

After this comes a highfalutin speech by Pandulpho, and cries of "Vindicta!" Balurdo, like the others, is so unreal that to deny his reality is to lend him too much existence; yet we can say of the scene, as of the play, that however bad it is no one but Marston could have written it.

The peculiar quality, which we have not attempted to define, is less evident in most of the plays which follow, just because they are better plays. The most considerable—setting aside his work of collaboration—are *The Malcontent, The Dutch Courtesan, The Insatiate Countess,* and *The Fawn.* Of these, the last is a slight but pleasant handling of an artificial situation, a kind of Courtship of Miles Standish in which the princess woos the prince who has come to sue on behalf of his father. The Insatiate Countess is a poor rival of the White Devil; her changes of caprice from lover to lover are rapid to the point of farce; and when the Countess, brought to the block for her sins, exclaims, in reply to the executioner's bidding of "Madam, put up your hair":

> *O, these golden nets*
> *That have ensnared so many wanton youths,*
> *Not one but has been held a thread of life,*
> *And superstitiously depended on.*
> *Now to the block we must vail. What else?*

we may remark (if these lines are indeed Marston's) that we have known this sort of thing done better by another dramatist, and that it is not worth going to Marston for what Webster can give us. *The Dutch Courtesan* is a better play than either of these; Freevill and Malheureux behave more naturally than we expect of Marston's heroes; the Courtesan's villainy is not incredible or unmotivated, and her isolation is enhanced by her broken English; and the heroine, Beatrice, has some charming verses to speak and is not, according to the standards of that stage and age, preposterously mild and patient. Yet the play as a whole is not particularly "signed" by Marston; it is a theme which might have been handled as well, or better, by Dekker or Heywood.

We are looking, not for plays of the same kind and in parts almost as good as those done by other dramatists. To prove that Marston is worth the attention of any but the Elizabethan scholar, we must convince the reader that Marston does something that no one else does at all: that there is a Marston tone, like the scent of a flower, which by its peculiarity sharpens our appreciation of the other dramatists as well as bringing appreciation of itself, as experiences of gardenia or zinnia refine our experience of rose or sweet-pea. With this purpose in mind, we may agree, with reservations, with the accepted view that *The Malcontent* is superior to any of the three other plays mentioned in the foregoing paragraph.

The superiority of *The Malcontent* does not lie altogether in more solid dramatic construction. The construction is hardly as close as that of *The Dutch Courtesan,* and the lighter passages have hardly the interest of under-plot which, in the other play, we find in the pranks played by Cocledemoy at the expense of Mulligrub. Marston at best is not a careful enough playwright to deserve comparison with his better-known contemporaries on this score. He can commit the grossest carelessness in confusing his own characters. Even in *The Malcontent* there appears to be one such lapse. Several of the earlier scenes seem to depend for their point upon Bianca being the wife of Bilioso (a sort of prototype of the Country Wife); but she is not so named in the list of characters, and the words of Ferneze to her in the last scene seem to indicate that Marston had forgotten this relationship.

Nor is the character of Malevole really comparable to that of Jacques. In the play of Shakespeare, Jacques is surrounded by characters who by their contrast with him, and sometimes by their explicit remarks, criticize the point of view which he expresses—a point of view which is indeed an almost consciously adopted humour. And while a malcontent drawn by Jonson lacks the depth and the variety which Shakespeare can give by human contrasts, he at least preserves a greater degree of consistency than does Malevole. The whole part is inadequately thought out; Malevole is either too important or not important enough. We may suppose that he has assumed his role primarily as a disguise, and in order to be present at his usurper's court on the easy footing of a tolerated eccentric. But he has the difficult role of being both the detached cynic and the rightful prince biding his time. He takes pity on Ferneze (himself not a very satisfying character, as after his pardon in Act IV he lets the play down badly in Act V, Sc. iii by his unseemly levity with Bianca). Yet Malevole, in his soliloquy in Act III, Sc. i, which is apparently not for the benefit of Bilioso but intended to express his true thoughts and feelings, alludes to himself as suffering from insomnia because he "'gainst his fate repines and quarrels"—not a philosophical role, nor one to be expected of the magnanimous duke whom he has to be at the end. Whether his sarcasms are meant to be affected railing or savage satire, they fail of their effect.

Nor is any of the other characters very much alive. It is possible to find Dr. Harrison's praise of Maria, as a "virtuous and constant wife who is alive and interesting," to be excessive, and to find even Maquerelle deficient in liveliness. The virtue of *The Malcontent,* indeed, resides rather in its freedom from the grosser faults to be expected of Marston than from any abundance of positive merits, when we hold it up to the standard, not of Shakespeare, but of the contemporaries of Shakespeare. It has no passages so moving as the confrontation of Beatrice and Franceschina in *The Dutch Courtesan,* and no comic element so sprightly as the harlequinades of Cocledemoy in the same play. It has, as critics have remarked, a more controlled and even diction. Swinburne does not elevate it to the position of Marston's best play; but he observes that

"the brooding anger, the resentful resignation, the impatient spirit of endurance, the bitter passion of disdain, which animate the utterance and direct the action of the hero, are something more than dramatically appropriate; it is as obvious that these are the mainsprings of the poet's own ambitions and dissatisfied intelligence, sullen in its reluctant submission and ardent in its implacable appeal, as that his earlier undramatic satires were the tumultuous and turbid ebullitions of a mood as morbid, as restless and as honest."

We are aware, in short, with this as with Marston's other plays, that we have to do with a positive, powerful, and unique personality. His is an original variation of that deep discontent and rebelliousness so frequent among the Elizabethan dramatists. He is, like some of the greatest of them, occupied in saying something else than appears in the literal actions and characters whom he manipulates.

It is possible that what distinguishes poetic drama from prosaic drama is a kind of doubleness in the action, as if it took place on two planes at once. In this it is different from allegory, in which the abstraction is something conceived, not something differently felt, and from symbolism (as in the plays of Maeterlinck) in which the tangible world is deliberately diminished—both symbolism and allegory being operations of the conscious planning mind. In poetic drama a certain apparent irrelevance may be the symptom of this doubleness; or the drama has an under-pattern, less manifest than the theatrical one. We sometimes feel, in following the words and behaviour of some of the characters of Dostoevsky, that they are living at once on the plane that we know and on some other plane of reality from which we are shut out: their behaviour does not seem crazy, but rather in conformity with the laws of some world that we cannot perceive. More fitfully, and with less power, this doubleness appears here and there in the work of Chapman, especially in the two *Bussy D'Ambois* plays. In the work of genius of a lower order, such as that of the author of *The*

Revenger's Tragedy, the characters themselves hardly attain this double reality; we are aware rather of the author, operating perhaps not quite consciously through them, and making use of them to express something of which he himself may not be quite conscious.

It is not by writing quotable "poetic" passages, but by giving us the sense of something behind, more real than any of his personages and their action, that Marston established himself among the writers of genius. There is one among his plays, not so far mentioned, and not, apparently, widely read or highly esteemed, which may be put forward with the claim that it is his best, and that it is the most nearly adequate expression of his distorted and obstructed genius: *The Wonder of Women,* otherwise *The Tragedy of Sophonisba.* This is a fairly late play in Marston's brief career, and we have reason to guess that the author himself preferred it to his others. As the "tragedy which shall boldly abide the most curious perusal," it gives the impression of being the play which Marston wrote most nearly to please himself. Bullen found it "not impressive," and even Swinburne reserves his praise for a few scenes. Yet the play has a good plot, is well constructed, and moves rapidly. There are no irrelevances and no comic passages; it is austere and economical. The rapidity with which the too-scheming Carthaginians transfer their allegiance from Massinissa to Syphax, his rival suitor for Sophonisba, bringing about an alliance between Massinissa and Scipio, is not unplausible, and keeps the reader in a state of con-

tinuous excitement over the fortunes of war. The
scene in which the witch Erictho takes on the form
of Sophonisba in order to induce Syphax to lie with
her, is by no means what Bullen would have it, a
scene of gratuitous horror, introduced merely to
make our flesh creep; it is integral to the plot of the
play; and is one of those moments of a double
reality, in which Marston is saying something else,
which evidence his poetic genius. And the memorable passages are not, as in his earlier plays, plums
imbedded in suet; they may be taken as giving a
fair taste of the quality of the whole play—*e.g.*

> *though Heaven bears*
> *A face far from us, gods have most long ears;*
> *Jove has a hundred marble marble hands.*

> *Nothing in Nature is unserviceable,*
> *No, not even inutility itself.*
> *Is then for nought dishonesty in being?*
> *And if it be sometimes of forced use,*
> *Wherein more urgent than in saving nations?*

> *Our vows, our faith, our oaths, why they're ourselves.*

> *Gods naught foresee, but see, for to their eyes*
> *Naught is to come or past; nor are you vile*
> *Because the gods foresee; for gods, not we*
> *See as things are; things are not as we see.*

(This last quotation reminds us of Meredith's line,
"By their great memories the gods are known"; but
Marston has the better of it. Swinburne, in spite of
his ability to like almost any Elizabethan play that

can be tolerated, is less than fair, when he calls *Sophonisba* "laboured and ambitious," and speaks of "jagged barbarisms and exotic monstrosities of metaphor"; and his derogatory quotation of the end of Act II does injustice to a passage which is acceptable enough in its context.)

I do not praise gods' goodness, but adore;
Gods cannot fall, and for their constant goodness
(Which is necessitated) they have a crown
Of never-ending pleasures. . . .

The following has a distinct originality:

Where statues and Jove's acts were vively limned
Boys with black coals draw the veil'd parts of nature,
And lecherous actions of imagin'd lust;
Where tombs and beauteous urns of well-dead men
Stood in assured rest, the shepherd now
Unloads his belly, corruption most abhorr'd
Mingling itself with their renowned ashes.

The following has a fine Senecal ring:

My god's my arm; my life my heaven; my grave
To me all end.

And the last words of Sophonisba,

He that ne'er laughed may with a constant face
Contemn Jove's frown: happiness makes us base.

may be considered as a "classical" comparison to the "romantic" vein of Tourneur's

I think man's happiest when he forgets himself.

It is hoped that the reader will see some justification for accumulating quotations from *Sophonisba,* and leaving the other plays unquoted. The quotations are intended to exhibit the exceptional consistency of texture of this play, and its difference of tone, not only from that of Marston's other plays, but from that of any other Elizabethan dramatist. In spite of the tumultuousness of the action, and the ferocity and horror of certain parts of the play, there is an underlying serenity; and as we familiarize ourselves with the play we perceive a pattern behind the pattern into which the characters deliberately involve themselves; the kind of pattern which we perceive in our own lives only at rare moments of inattention and detachment, drowsing in sunlight. It is the pattern drawn by what the ancient world called Fate; subtilized by Christianity into mazes of delicate theology; and reduced again by the modern world into crudities of psychological or economic necessity.

We may be asked to account, in giving this play such high place, for the fact that neither contemporary popularity nor the criticism of posterity yields any support. Well; it may be modestly suggested that in our judgments of Elizabethan plays in general we are very much influenced by Elizabethan standards. The fact that Shakespeare transcended all other poets and dramatists of the time imposes a Shakespearian standard: whatever is of the same kind of drama as Shakespeare's, whatever may be measured by Shakespeare, however inferior to Shakespeare's it may be, is assumed to be better than whatever is of a different kind. However catholic-minded we may be in general, the moment we enter the Elizabethan period we praise or condemn plays according to the usual Elizabethan criteria. Fulke Greville has never received quite his due; we approach Greville, and Daniel, with the assumption that they are "not in the main current." The minor poet who hitches his skiff astern of the great galleon has a better chance of survival than the minor poet who chooses to paddle by himself. Marston, in the one play on which he appears to have prided himself, is Senecal rather than Shakespearian. Had the great ship been that of a Corneille or a Racine, instead of a Shakespeare, Marston might cut a better figure now. He spent nearly the whole of his dramatic career writing a kind of drama against which we feel that he rebelled. In order to enjoy the one play which he seems to have written to please himself, we should read Greville and Daniel, of his affinity with whom he was probably quite unconscious, and we should come to him fresh from Corneille and Racine. He would, no doubt, have shocked the French dramatists by his improprieties, and the English classicists as well: nevertheless, he should be with them, rather than with the Shakespearians.